ETHICS AND THE ENVIRONMENT

Edited by

Richard E. Hart
Bloomfield College

UNIVERSITY
PRESS OF
AMERICA

Lanham • New York • London

The
Long Island
Philosophical
Society

Library of Congress Cataloging-in-Publication Data

Ethics and the environment / edited by Richard E. Hart.
p.   cm.
Papers originally presented at a conference held on the C.W. Post
Campus of Long Island University, Apr. 13, 1985, sponsored by the
Long Island Philosophical Society.
Includes bibliographical references.
1. Human ecology—Moral and ethical aspects—Congresses.
2. Human ecology—New York (State)—Long Island—Moral and
ethical aspects—Congresses.   I. Hart, Richard E., 1949–
II. Long Island Philosophical Society.
GF80.E842   1992   179'.1—dc20   92–15151 CIP

ISBN 0–8191–8512–4 (cloth : alk. paper)
ISBN 0–8191–8513–2 (pbk. : alk. paper)

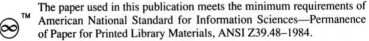

The paper used in this publication meets the minimum requirements of
American National Standard for Information Sciences—Permanence
of Paper for Printed Library Materials, ANSI Z39.48–1984.

For My Mother and Father

Norma J. Hart
Victor T. Hart, Jr.

TABLE OF CONTENTS

Case Analyses: Long Island Problems

Nuclear Energy and the Environment

Safe Water Supply

PREFACE

The papers that comprise this volume were originally presented at the Conference on Ethics and the Environment, held on the C.W. Post Campus of Long Island University April 13, 1985. Most papers have subsequently undergone revision and updating prior to their appearance here. The Conference was the first ever of its kind on Long Island and the first general conference on a theme in "applied philosophy" to be sponsored by the Long Island Philosophical Society. A few words concerning the origin and shaping of the Conference are in order prior to a number of acknowledgements.

By the early 1980's the Long Island Philosophical Society was just over twenty years old. It was an association of philosophers and students of philosophy from area colleges and universities that met twice annually on a local campus. Papers were read, panels convened and occasionally a notable speaker from outside would be invited to give an address. Around 1982 the Executive Committee of the Society resolved to invigorate the organization by seeking to sponsor larger events that were at once relevant to members but, also, connected to broader concerns of philosophical research or emerging social issues. Optimistically, the Society even contemplated the possible publication of the proceedings of such conferences as yet another way of gaining visibility and additional support.

vii

To its good fortune the Society was able to secure some generous private donations expressly dedicated to support the staging of an occasional large conference and underwrite some of the costs of publishing the proceedings. The first such large event, the Conference on Socrates, took place in the fall of 1983, and attracted contributors and participants from throughout the New York region and as far away as Virginia, Pennsylvania and Ohio. The Conference featured Greek scholar, Eric Havelock, and was published as a volume under the title *New Essays on Socrates* (UPA, 1984), edited by Eugene Kelly. The second such conference was the Conference on Ethics and the Environment in 1985. The third major event occurred in 1987, the Conference on Professional Ethics in Health Care Services, hosted by the New York Chiropractic College. This unique gathering, which featured a keynote address by noted philosopher Michael Bayles of Florida State University, sought to bring together (perhaps for the first time) philosophers specializing in ethical analysis with a variety of members of the non-allopathic health professions to examine ethical issues that arise in these professions. The resulting published proceedings, under the same title as the Conference, was again edited by Eugene Kelly (UPA, 1988).

The Conference on Ethics and the Environment, however, was the first to be dedicated wholly to an issue in the realm of applied philosophy and the first to be interdisciplinary in its structure. It coincided with a rapid, nation-wide evolution in philosophical research, teaching and writing into areas like business and medical ethics, public policy planning, feminism, critical thinking skills and multiculturalism. Several members of the Long Island Philosophical Society, who later became the Organizing Committee for the Conference, had at that time become more and more interested in areas of applied ethics and issues pertaining to environment and technology. They, also, recognized that different perspectives and methodologies beyond philosophy—scientific, legal, political—were needed in order to properly address environmental concerns. So the Conference itself—its timing and its multi-disciplinary, multi-professional focus—was neither accident nor coincidence. What was desperately needed, the Committee believed, was, on the one hand, facts, data, scientific and legal analyses, political agendas, and, on the other, exploration of the value implications and the interrelations between ethical principles, scientific evidence, legal precedents, and political responses. The basic goal was to initiate dialogue across disciplinary and professional boundaries, rather than have a group of philosophers speak exclusively to other philosophers. The diverse nature of program contributors, the audience that turned out, the reporting of the event in the local media, and various forms of oral and written feedback, all suggested that the goal of beginning discussion had been more than achieved.

Several acknowledgments and expressions of gratitude are necessary. The task of structuring and scheduling the Conference, reading papers, and inviting speakers, fell to the Organizing Committee. In addition to myself, as chair, it consisted of Dr. Harold Allen, Adelphi University, Dr. Maureen Feder-Marcus, State University of New York at Old Westbury, Dr. Eugene Kelly, New York Institute of Technology, and Dr. Evelyn Shirk, Hofstra University. Special thanks are owing to the then-officers of the Society — Dr. Eugene Kelly, Executive Secretary and Professor Daphne McKinney, Treasurer — for their support and assistance. The Conference would never have been realized except for the good offices of the administration and staff of the C.W. Post Campus of Long Island University, with special thanks to student assistants Karen Berjaron and Steve Morales.

On the technical side, in terms of manuscript preparation, a great debt is owed to Stanley Silverman, his staff, and Dr. Eugene Kelly, all of the New York Institute of Technology, for generous amounts of their time and skill in initial scanning and editing of the papers. Jamileh Amirzafari of the Talbott Library, Bloomfield College, helped with preparation of the Bibliography. Colleague John Towsen, of Bloomfield's Fine and Performing Arts Program, provided valuable technical advice. And Carole A. Kokotowski, the person most instrumental in preparing final copy, is deserving of high praise for her generosity of spirit, promptness, technical expertise, and patience with me and my style of editing. The occasion should not pass, also, without extending thanks, on behalf of the Executive Committee of the Long Island Philosophical Society, to Oscar and Beatrice Bekoff and the late Dr. Ernest G. Napalitano for their generous support of the Society and its work. My gratitude is also extended to Bloomfield College for awarding me a "study leave" for fall 1991, and to the Department of Philosophy at the State University of New York at Stony Brook for providing me a position as Research Associate during the period of the leave. The support and inspiration of friends and colleagues at both institutions has aided my work.

Finally, the job of editor, I have discovered, is as difficult as it is, at times, thankless. The good side of it, however, is that it puts one in close collaboration with a number of fine colleagues. To all those whose contributions appear in this volume, to all who attended or helped to bring about the Conference, and those who followed up with me in various ways afterward, I offer my special thanks and appreciation. For all, both on Long Island and beyond, who care about the natural environment and are dedicated to studied reflection and effective action relating to environmental concerns, I can only hope this book provides some measure of clarity and insight. Needless to say, whatever shortcomings, errors or omissions may exist are my sole responsibility.

Richard E. Hart
Smithtown, Long Island
Fall 1991

INTRODUCTION

"Environmental Ethics: General Issues and Long Island Problems"

By Richard E. Hart
Bloomfield College

The papers in this volume seek to enhance understanding and action, relating to environmental matters, in a variety of ways. One way is accentuation of the age-old theory and practice controversy. From the time of Socrates and the Greeks to Marx and Engels, the pragmatism and instrumentalism of Dewey, and the present-day thrust toward "applied philosophy", philosophers have continuously wrestled with the question of how to properly conceive the relationship between theory and practice. Is there, for example, pure understanding, of a theoretical sort, wholly separate from action, rather like that described to me in a recent chance meeting with a mathematician who proclaimed his work to be purely theoretical and, thus, not connected to the practical world or to people's lives (ironically, however, much of his research funding is provided by the armed forces)? Or, as some political activists might have us believe, is the quest for understanding and theory simply an impediment to action? Should we simple engage in praxis and later perhaps try to make sense of things in some broader theoretical fashion? Surely, the growing work in the specialized areas of applied ethics (medical, business, journalistic, environmental) has pressed home the idea of a synthesis or blending of theory and practice wherein it makes little sense to speak of "pure" theory or "pure" practice or to conceive of their relatedness as theory *vs.* practice. Theory and understanding is always a prerequisite to reasonable and effective action — whether in ethics, politics, scientific experimentation or artistic creation — just as action serves as a prime demonstration or instantiation of the results of theorizing and understanding. Professor Shirk summarizes a key assumption characteristic of all the work in this volume when in her essay she states, "All ethical practice is guided by theory and all ethical theory has practice as its ultimate destination."

Bearing this in mind, it is important to note that the entire realm of what has come to be known as "applied philosophy" represents a significant challenge to contemporary philosophizing. Just as, in the nineteenth century, Frederich Nietzsche was said to have turned Western philosophy and religion on its head, so has "applied philosophy" in important ways brought about re-thinking, modifications and extensions in the analytic, continental and American modes of philosophizing that have characterized the twentieth century. Perhaps more in the spirit of the American social tradition of Dewey and James than other modes and styles, "applied philosophy" has led philosophers of all stripes into areas like public policy planning, curriculum reform, government and military assignments, health care decision making, and the management chambers of corporate America. Simply put, "applied philosophy" has grown enormously in currency and value. Accordingly, it has added considerable new life to the branches of philosophy that fall under the rubrics ethics, social and political, and decision theory, and helped make these areas far more respectable, both inside the university and out, than perhaps ever before. A quick survey of publishers' catalogues and new journals, or of the specialty groups and societies that increasingly factor into the national programs of the American Philosophical Association, provides ample evidence for this claim. At its best "applied philosophy" represents the successful wedding of philosophical methodologies and concepts, both traditional and contemporary, with issues and concerns that are crucial to the age in which we live. The reader will discover numerous examples of such wedding included in this volume.

The focus on theory and practice, and the long-standing debate over their relation, reminds us of the critical importance of our intellectual and philosophical heritage. Today's reflection and activity must be informed by an understanding of the past, lest, as Santayana reminded us, our ignorance of history dooms us to repeat the mistakes of the past. Essays in this volume by Soupios, Shirk and Berleant reflect on philosophical history, and seek to demonstrate the bearing of earlier concepts and notions on our comprehension of ethics and ecological consciousness today. Western philosophical speculation originated, as exemplified in Empedocles, in a focus on the elements of nature (earth, air, fire and water). But, as Soupios demonstrates, on close examination the Greeks did not seem to hold a viable concept of ecology or even a healthy respect for nature. For the Greeks man was the centerpiece, and his goals and purposes took precedence, a theme picked up, indeed, exacerbated in the later thought of Francis Bacon.

The work of Mooney, Sprintzen, Katz and Walther aids understanding and action by clarifying, critically analyzing and applying key philosophic, economic and political concepts such as property rights, intrinsic and instrumental value, "community" vs. "organism" models of nature, social costs and social strategy. What do these notions mean? What are their implications, and how are they related to environmental concerns? The sharpening of these notions helps provide a steadier focus on the environmental crisis and what can and should be done in response to it.

Philosophic reflection on the environment is crucial, yet it does not provide a complete portrait. Political and legislative, scientific and technical perspectives, also, factor largely in the understanding of environmental issues. County Executive Halpin's address identifies a "second generation" of challenges to the environment and outlines a number of political and legislative measures — some accomplished, some still on the agenda — that attack environmental problems head-on. It asks: what practical steps in the areas of regulation and governance will positively effect people's daily lives, and what ethical considerations are involved in taking such steps? Goldfarb, Kluewer, Watson and Kane provide technical and scientific, as well as ethical, analyses of two environmental issues of considerable importance to Long Island (and the world), nuclear power stations, and the risk of accidents, and the availability of fresh groundwater supplies. While the papers offer historical accounts of the nuclear power industry and of numerous studies involving groundwater, technical data and history are linked inextricably to ethical evaluation and public policy decisions. The reader, thus, returns full circle to the union of theory and practice.

Roughly half of the essays in this volume, the political and scientific pieces, are written with a focus on Long Island, New York. Like suburban, bedroom communities in major metropolitan areas throughout the country, Long Island's rapid population and commercial growth following World War II brought with it an abundance of negative environmental effects. In this regard, Long Island is very much a microcosm of the macrocosm. But, as our authors remind us, Long Island is a uniquely constituted area as well. Geographically, it is, of course, surrounded by water, water that seriously limits access to and exit from the Island, water that is central to commerce and recreation, and water that has become increasingly spoiled by offshore dumping, accidental spills and dramatic increases in recreational boating. Geologically, it is a fragile, sandy strip of land in the ocean, with a fresh water aquifer relatively close to the surface and lying beneath the most industrialized area of the Island. Ecologically, it has lots of extremely sensitive wetlands areas, where shellfish are forever at risk, and thousands of acres of virgin pine barrens that developers covet for their purposes. So it is both similar and different in relation to the sorts of environmental problems that beset the industrialized world. Clearly, it is an excellent lens through which to better understand and tackle such problems.

Long Island has been forced to deal with problems of groundwater contamination, the solid waste landfill crisis, beach and surf pollution, the possibility of nuclear accident, and deteriorating air quality. From the standpoint of long-term threats to the environment, it has unfortunately become a rather classic example of American development and its attendant effects. Simultaneously, however, Long Island has innovated and frequently led the nation in the attempted resolution of environmental problems. This includes radical wetlands preservation programs, passage of a bottle return bill in 1981, public acquisition of many tracts of pine barrens, and large-scale closure of landfills. To be more specific, the Environmental Defense Fund, today one of the nation's premiere environmental groups, originated in Stony Brook, Long Island in 1969 as a result of concerns about the pesticide DDT. In 1984 Suffolk County banned smoking in most public places. In spring of 1990 the County considered a bill that would compell newspaper companies to use recycled newsprint in all of their papers by the end of 1996, a measure much stricter than other such measures under consideration around the country. In June of 1991 Hofstra University convened and hosted a major interdisciplinary conference entitled "The Environment: Global Politics — Local Solutions." In June 1991, despite Suffolk's bleak financial outlook, lawmakers approved final bonding of $50 million to purchase pine barrens under the County's Clean Drinking Water Protection Program. And at a time when universities are cutting programs and curricula is increasingly oriented toward high technology and employment, Long Island's Adelphi University has in the fall of 1991 introduced a new, multidisciplinary Environmental Studies Program, an initiative that hopes to add to the resolution of the world environment's complex problems by addressing such problems from the standpoints of science, law, public health, business and individual behavior. Not to be lost in all this is the fact that is recent years Long Islanders were able to bind together and block the opening of the Shoreham nuclear power plant principally because of major concerns over a workable evacuation plan in the event of an accident. Donald J. Middleton, former Long Island regional director for the state Department of Environmental Conservation, summed up the past ten years of environmental initiatives on Long Island in these words:

> The federally funded "208" program aimed at protecting our water supply is largely in place and the pine barrens are well on the way to preservation. The total environmental protection budget has increased significantly. The quantity of our drinking water is by and large stabilized and the quality of our drinking water is better protected than any sole-source aquifer system in the world.

> We Long Islanders have successfully invested a nationally precedent-setting $500 million in five resource recovery plants to burn more than half of our garbage and generate electricity. We're ahead of any major community in America in getting out of the garbage landfill business. And, as a community, we are approaching a record-setting recycling participation level.[1]

Unquestionably in the past 20 to 25 years there has been considerable public awakening and genuine progress in relation to environmental threats both on Long Island and throughout the country. But everyone knows that challenges and dangers, both real and potential, still exist all around us. As this book was being completed in July 1991 I was in northern California when a train derailment dumped 19,000 gallons of metham sodium, a fumigant used to sterilize soil, into the Sacramento River. It devastated 45 miles of the river and the 11 mile-long toxic spill, labeled "green death", eventually moved into Shasta Lake. Six weeks later more than 100 people along the river were still suffering symptoms and reports of miscarriages, possibly related to the chemical, were beginning to appear.[2] Whereas Halpin in his essay speaks of "second generation" environmental crises, some like Middleton are beginning to speak of "third generation" risks. For instance, it is imperative that we now face up to the elimination of *all* forms of illegal dumping, including the dumping of sewage sludge in the oceans. Now that incineration is becoming a more widely used mode of waste disposal, we must apply the resources of science and technology to methods of burning that do not transfer pollutants to the air. Closely tied to this, on Long Island and elsewhere, is the radical movement toward permanent closure of landfills. Such closures have contributed to the growing incidence of transferring garbage and incinerated ash across state lines to dumping grounds in remote, usually poor, areas of the country. Obviously, a tremendous bind exists here. As *Newsday* reported in a recent feature story, as a result of state-mandated landfill closures — and despite slowly expanding recycling programs — areas like New York City and Long Island "...are still as dependent on out-of-state disposal as a junkie is on a fix. In fact New York and New Jersey ship more garbage and incinerator ash across state lines — more than 1000 truckloads daily — than the other 48 states combined."[3] Like most environmental issues, the situation is ambiguous and divisive — large metropolitan areas desperately need places to dispose of potentially dangerous waste while poor areas of the country desperately need the revenue from shipping fees and garbage taxes in order to maintain school systems and other public services. Spotlighting the dilemma, the same *Newsday* feature discussed a recent proposal by a subsidiary of Torrington, Connecticut based O. and G. Industries, Inc. to build the largest landfill in the United States at a site on the Rosebud Sioux Reservation in the badlands of South Dakota. As one might expect, the Indian community is deeply divided over whether their "sacred" land should be used for such purposes, while fully recognizing that the additional revenue would help ameliorate their long-standing situation of chronic poverty and alcoholism.

So what dictates the resolution of these issues? Should the criteria be jobs and economic gain, ethical correctness, public health, or preservation of the integrity of nature? The answers are, of course, difficult and seemingly elusive. But those who have contributed to this volume — philosophers, scientists, politicians, humanists — all realize that environmental issues will not go away and are, at base, matters of common concern. They affect all of us. Though we all generate larger than necessary amounts of garbage, today we are confronted with the NIMBY (Not In My

Back Yard) syndrome, or, even more radically, the BANANA (Build Absolutely Nothing Anywhere Near Anybody) movement. But can we afford the luxury of such positions any longer? Since we are all culpable in some measure, must we not all take responsibility for the environment, for our waste generation and disposal, and not simply ship the problems off elsewhere? While the authors in this collection have not provided definitive answers, they have vigorously defined the mutuality of the environmental situation and contributed to an urgent dialogue. They have demonstrated, through their examples, the overriding need to bring to bear the expertise and values of each and all to problems of the environment, and to come to the table, so to speak, in a spirit of cooperation, honesty and community.

NOTES

[1]Donald J. Middleton, "L.I. Faces Environmental Choices", *Newsday*, September 20, 1991, p. 129.

[2]c.f. *USA Today*, "Toxic Spill Seeps Into Reservoir", July 18, 1991 and *Newsday*, "A Toxic Cloud's Legacy of Fear In California", August 28, 1991.

[3]Dan Fagin, "Badlands in Demand", *Newsday*, October 21, 1991, p. 5.

NEW DIMENSIONS IN ETHICS:
ETHICS AND THE ENVIRONMENT[1]

By Evelyn Shirk
Hofstra University

The past decade or so has brought considerable change to the scope and application of ethics. Ethics moved out of the halls of academe, out of the cathedral and entered the market place. Public and private attention turned to large social problems of action and practice, flooding the media and publishers' catalogues and dominating random chatter. Controversies over abortion, capital punishment, mercy killings, the treatment of animals, the behavior of Congressmen, the morality of medical practice, and the decisions of researchers captured attention. The changes were swift and extensive. I hardly think that any of us who teach ethics were more than vaguely aware of what was happening, since "becoming aware" is a long-term process involving many levels of comprehension.

Swimming with the tide, academia followed suit, responding with a rash of new courses. *Professional Ethics, Medical Ethics, Business Ethics, Contemporary Ethical Dilemmas, Ethics and Technology* began to replace the standard student fare of *Theories of Value, Histories of Ethics and Readings in Ethical Theory.* Students flocked to these hot new items in droves. A new brand of intellectuals called "Ethicists" appeared, claiming expertise in vexing practical decisions. Committees on ethics took up habitation in hospitals, in Congress and in laboratory complexes. (Some say

1

to dilute blame for unfortunate decisions.) Ethics lost its reputation for peddling routine platitudes and grew in favor and stature with the American public as never before. Ethics had taken a so-called "practical turn" with a vengeance, and the name, "Practical Ethics", was used to distinguish the new enterprise from what was apparently thought to be an earlier over-enthusiasm with theory. As usual, it was foolishly named. All ethical practice is guided by theory and all ethical theory has practice as its ultimate destination.

Reasons for this new and extended interest in practice are not difficult to assign. Almost all of it has grown out of the development of some corner of technology which brought radical changes to our life and times. Technology has been growing exponentially, bringing with it a plethora of events deeply important for human welfare. Pushing ahead on every front, technology has increasingly been able to change, modify and transform our environment, thus presenting us with an ever different world in which to act and choose. It has brought new implements, instruments, machines and processes; new fabrics, fibers and building materials; new medical capabilities, new pesticides and defoliants; new paints, solvents and glues; it has brought the computer, the laser and the transistor and a whole array of electronic products; it has brought new nuclear applications for both peace and war, new and exotic biological and genetic research and an absolutely staggering amount of by-products, waste and debris which only gradually began to be recognized as both troublesome and dangerous.

It began to be clear that our technological prowess was beginning to have an incalculable effect on our lives, our culture and on God's green earth. Environmental Ethics, as distinct from all other varieties of practical ethics, was born. Not that any discipline is born full formed from the Head of Jove, nor that it is immediately recognized as an independent inquiry. As John Herman Randall used to say, it takes time for a series of issues, problems and questions to coagulate enough around a common core to be recognized as a discrete discipline. But Environmental Ethics is not only a separate inquiry: I hope to show that it has distinctive differences with other types of practical ethics; that it is, in fact, a dimensional variation of traditional ethical inquiry. Other types of practical ethics, with the exception, perhaps, of ethics pertaining to animals, can more or less rely on the accumulated concepts and convictions of historical ethics, for a start, at least. Environmental Ethics can take no such comfort, as I shall try to show. Unlike other new applications of ethics to practice, the inquirer into

2

ethics of the environment is challenged to uncover its particular assumptions, to delineate its theoretical framework and to pinpoint its differences with traditional ethical concepts.

It's a big order — to be undertaken only by brash natures. It requires generalization, and generalization invites citations of omissions and exceptions. Yet nothing less is adequate to guide the future policies and practices of this new, and perhaps fateful, area of ethical application. At bottom, Environmental Ethics is morality confronting technology head on and holding it accountable.

Environmental Ethics is about choices and decisions we make which affect the environment and hence affect human life. To what do we refer when we speak of "the" environment? We live in many types of environments. We live in a social, a political, an economic and a psychic environment, to mention only a few. Apparently "the" environment identifies our so-called "physical" surroundings as more fundamental and basic than any of the others, and with good reason. As Santayana aptly put it, "Spirit cannot fly without material wings." Nor is our reference to "Mother" earth specious. It is indeed the source and caretaker of our being. The physical environment, which consists of bodies, forces and processes, is what used to be called "Nature" as distinct from human nature. A passing but important question here is whether our own bodies are part of our physical environment in the above sense. I am inclined to think that they are — at least from one point of view. Yet from another point of view, this pushes us into a body/mind dualism not sustained by evidence. And it leaves us with Descartes' insoluble problem of accounting for interaction, unless, of course, we no longer consider "mind" as a type of entity but as a set of functions. I will leave this aspect of the matter for you to consider.

Now one hardly needs reflection to realize that the substantive meanings of the term "environment" have already had a long history with yet more detail and complexity to come. What we mean by the term is entirely dependent on the level of our scientific sophistication. The simple, ancient description of the environment as consisting of earth, air, fire and water has gained infinite elaboration across the centuries as theoretical knowledge proliferated and technical know-how followed apace. I invite you to reflect on the amount of detail which each term of that simple series has accumulated across the centuries.

3

Yet in us lurk a number of anachronisms which seem to persist in our contemporary thinking. For a long time in human history, nature was understood to be stable, its cyclical changes unalterable, its capacities enduringly there and impervious to our presence. It could be relied upon to quench thirst, grow food, disperse the smoke from fires and provide materials for shelter, regardless of our human activities. And for some denizens of the twentieth century, these convictions still persist.

Furthermore, our nurturing "mother" was previously understood to be self-rejuvenating. She could be counted on to regrow her forests despite the woodsman, purify her streams despite the dumpster, restock her lakes despite the fisherman and replenish the land with animals despite the huntsman. And so she did. This vision of nature as a self-sustaining, self-renewing paradise abounds in literature and poetry (I think of Emerson and Thoreau). Even our infatuation with "the natural" in general and "natural" foods in particular seems oblivious of the present impossibility of food untouched by the hand of man's technology. We still open the window to obtain "fresh air" and we swim for "healthful" refreshment. We seem to have forgotten that paradise has been lost. Our amnesia left us open to shock and astonishment when we discovered the havoc which radiation can wreak on air, water, soil and living tissue; when we learned of newly constructed viruses which could wipe out the world's population and when we found out that acid rain had spread its lethal effects around the world. Yet these awesome facts were relatively remote and incomprehensible to American minds compared to actual encounter with thousands of toxic dump sites oozing their poisons into the homeowner's basement. The earth, which once seemed so reliably able to nurture humanity, now threatened sickness and death to a frightened population. The heavens which once seemed so serene, distant and pure enough to house the gods, now threaten us with falling space labs and assorted man-made debris. Even the earth's climate, formally believed to be in God's hands, is now understood to be altered by the aerosol can. Long held convictions regarding the natural environment have a stubborn persistence. In a "throw-away" society, we have yet to understand that there *is* no place called "away". Our present perspective on the environment consists of an inconsistent welter of new facts and old convictions.

As the century unfolded and these events penetrated our reluctant consciousness, they bred a new and dramatic sense of our dependence on

4

the earth and they fixed in us an urgent imperative to make our existence less problematical.

Let us turn to classical ethics in order to highlight some ways in which Environmental Ethics is different from its ancestry. First, before technology's meteoric rise to power and prestige, ethics had little truck with the physical environment which was simply there to be used and enjoyed. The thrust of classical ethics was on the self, on its personal excellence and on its happiness and fulfillment. And even though, for Aristotle, ethics was a branch of politics, his ethics centered on ways for the individual to achieve "eudymonia" or specifically *human* excellence. In the same spirit the Stoics sought a prescription for tranquility enough to permit the self to ride out life's storms while the pleasure seekers sought safe passage by means of a life of pleasurable forgetfulness.

In sharp contrast, Environmental Ethics is a group ethics, centered not on the self but on the human community as it interacts with a shared physical world — a world no longer fixed and static but one which we can change for better or worse; a world whose fate we all share. Its central concern is with the results of group choices which fall on all collectively. Environmental Ethics forgoes the luxury of pursuing happiness, recognizing the stark fact that physical survival takes precedence over all else in the order of ethical concerns, despite whatever martyrdom we subsequently contemplate. And in these new terms, personal welfare is inexorably linked to group welfare. Environmental catastrophe is no respecter of persons.

In its own terms, religious ethics, always present and active on the ethical scene, also centered its attention on the individual self in search of salvation, typically providing a set of exercises for the physical fitness of the individual soul. Religious ethics aims to gain favor in the eyes of God in order to ultimately inhabit a Celestial City, presumably unplagued by smog.

Environmental Ethics recognized quite clearly that man, not God, has caused our present distress. It seems clear that having eaten the forbidden fruit and opened the sealed box, we have little justification in appealing to God for help. We had opted for power and domination over nature and, having gained it, we hold nature's fate in our own hands. Environmental Ethics steadfastly affirms man's responsibility to maintain the viability of

5

the physical world as a habitation for genus *homo*. On its welfare rests the fate of the entire tribe.

As historical ethics began to be more alive to its interpersonal involvements, Kant examined the foundations of the moral law to which all rational beings are subject. Since all humans are capable of hearing the voice of conscience, Kantian ethics focussed on the interplay between men of good will. The principles which should govern anyone's actions had to be tested by means of their potential use by all. The thrust was on the metaphysical ground for rational interpersonal behavior.

In contrast to other forms of practical ethics, Environmental Ethics moves ethics for the first time from a personal and interpersonal context to a physical and global one. With that move a new and unprecedented player, the physical world, appears on the ethical stage. The physical world itself takes on ethical significance and plays a moral role. It has a moral claim on human attention and we have responsibility to it for three reasons. First, because we alter the environment in ways that are better or worse, we implant our morality in it. The environment is a recipient of our ethical choices regarding it, which are incorporated within its functioning. Second, the physical world mutely bears testimony to the quality of those choices which it transmits to the human community. I am not saying that because we are moral creatures, the physical world gains moral significance by some mysterious osmosis through contact with us. I am saying that the environment in *fact* relates to us by conveying the import of the choices of each to all. It reflects the moral quality of our acts. For example, a magnificent recreational lake brought to biological death and wearing a mottled shroud of dead fish because of a paper company's ceaseless dumping of sludge into its waters, speaks accurately and eloquently to all of the moral choices which brought it to this pass.

Third, the environment acts as a third party, a kind of moral medium of exchange between I and thou, transmitting the moral quality of my environmental choices to you and yours to me. It becomes a quasi-human participant in the consequences of our actions and is therefore more than what the scientist examines and more than his test tube and microscope reveal. Environmental Ethics thus changes the classical ethical duo of I and thou into a trio. I and thou become ethically related by means of the environment. And insofar as the physical world is more enduring than the individual self, it also transmits our choices to future generations as well.

6

The ethical trio now becomes a chorus since all humans, past, present and future inhabit the same limited globe. The stinking, rat-filled "sanitary landfills," complete with barrels of toxic chemicals, will unmistakably communicate the quality of our moral choices to our children. Waste oil pumped into the recesses of the earth will, without doubt, affect our grandchildren's drinking water (if not ours), while atomic waste buried in the earth's rock strata will be a problem for the life and health of distant future generations.

New ethical terms seem to be required for this new type of human relationship which emerges from our sharing the same world through the effects of our actions on that world. Environment-derived moral relations between us are different from other types of interpersonal ones. For instance, the contaminator doesn't harm us directly; he harms the physical world. Yet he indirectly harms us and all others. What shall we call his offense? On what grounds can he be accused and tried? And how is offense to be dealt with when the offender is a corporation or an accidental collection of manufacturing plants producing acid rain? How is the offense to be handled when the offender is a town, a state or the federal government? How, in traditional ethical terms, can we give meaning to the conviction that recycling or using renewable energy sources are deeply "moral" activities? How, in traditional terms, can we speak of "debts" to future generations? Only within a new perspective which recognizes that we are morally related to a non-human physical world can this notion make sense.

New terms, other than those used by the physical scientist, are also needed to describe the physical world. As a moral and not just physical relator of human kind, the physical world transcends its physicality. Proof of this transfiguration can be found in the character of our descriptions of these relations. We speak of "hurting" or of "benefitting" the environment; of "polluting" and "rescuing" it; of "nurturing" or "exploiting" it and even of "respecting" its "integrity." One environmental group calls itself, "Friends of the Earth." Such talk is neither anthropomorphic nor metaphorical. It truly expresses that we are, *in fact*, in a moral relation to the non-human world, a relation which might be described as something akin to a virus. A virus seems to be a half-way house between living and non-living entities. So the physical world is a halfway house between human and non-human entities. It takes on human traits when we view it in relation

7

to us and non-human ones when we examine it under the scientist's microscope.

Perhaps a clue to understanding this strange quasi-moral being with which we are in moral relation can be found in reconsidering just how we and the environment are physically related. The environment was once thought of as "out there" and "around" us — as separate and distinct from us. But a little reflection will reveal that it can no longer be thought of in this manner. Its air is *in* our lungs, its soil nutrients (or pollutants) compose our bodies; its rain is the water of which, in large part, our bodies are made. The earth's climate has shaped us and colored our skin. Far from being "out there," it is part of us. We and the physical environment co-mingle. Only by abstraction is the environment "outside." For the new inquiry, the old inner/outer dualisms are doomed to extinction. They have to give way to the realization that the larger context of "the world" includes both us and our physical environment in reciprocal relations which are both physical and moral.

This new perception that our relations to a physical world are not only physical but moral, as well, requires a wider conception of the moral self. The moral self was once seen as a creature of a time and place, responsible to itself reflexively and to other humans interactively. But with the new awareness of the self's *moral* relations with a *physical* world, the self gains an extended life. The physical world which is more enduring than the transient self receives and carries the effects of those choices to the not-yet-born. Our progeny will inherit the effects of our actions; they will experience the morality or lack of it in our inter-environmental relations. The quality of their lives will be determined by how and in what ways we have changed the soil, air and water of the future; how we have changed the flora and fauna. The moral self and its obligations thus extend across time. It becomes related to a succession of selves which its action affects. The biological continuum becomes a moral one, as well. While this may be old hat to the biologist, it is surely new to the ethical inquirer.

A new list of moral virtues enters ethics which evokes images of quite a different sort from the more familiar interpersonal ones. To be beneficent toward the biosphere, - i.e., Thou shalt not erode, pollute, poison, irradiate or make ugly is quite distinct from Thou shalt not kill, covet, deceive or steal. To respect our physical environment is quite different from respecting our neighbor. Yet the new set of unfamiliar

8

human excellences must sooner or later take their place beside the older, more familiar, interpersonal ones.

Environmental Ethics, as a discipline and an area of inquiry is subject to its own special types of problems which no previous ethics has had to confront. Many of these will be addressed by the papers to be presented here today. I had best leave these for others to explore. But before closing, let me say some things in celebration of this new discipline. Emerging in the second half of this century, Environmental Ethics seems to be fine compensation for the barrenness and unproductivity of much of the ethics of the first half. It has dispersed the pessimism and nihilism of those who seriously believed ethical choice to be no more than a wayward effusion of sentiment and those who earnestly believed that ethical choice would not be warranted by factual evidence. Morality confronting technology put an end to all of that. The idle games of the detractors of ethics and its reasoning processes came to an abrupt halt. Practical ethics revived contemporary ethics which was foundering in abstractions. All other types of practical ethics are extensions of classical ethics, using its insights and answers to illuminate new, interpersonal problems which technology brought to medicine, to the business world, to research centers. Environmental Ethics stands alone as a new and different practical inquiry. To be sure, it also extends interpersonal ethics, but it is a breed apart owing to the role played by the physical world. As a discipline, it requires the delineation of its new perspective and an outlining of its new categories.

The "practical turn" in ethics has performed some invaluable services for ethics in general. First, whether we would or not, it has pushed us headlong into a consequential ethics as against one dominated by Kantian-style rule. Second, its very nature demands a contextual framework within which our more naive dualisms (such as the is/ought dualism) dissolve. Third, it has brought home the realization that standards are man-made, shaped and designed by us to be scales upon which we weigh the outcomes of our choices. And it has forced us to accept the concept of good as more fundamental to ethics than that of right. Neither moral law nor civil law can keep pace with our exploding technology. Only good, with its heavy biological overtones, can measure progress in this domain.

In conclusion, Environmental Ethics, as a dimensional variation of ethics requires courage of its practitioners. It must confront deeply serious and perplexing group problems without rules to consult and without mottos and shibboleths to comfort. It is a discipline with few precedents and less history. Environmental Ethics is an inquiry which has to construct itself, has to identify its problems, reshape its own categories, forge its own reasons, and evaluate its own solutions. We are here to make a start.

NOTE

[1]Originally published, in slightly different form, in *The Journal of Value Inquiry* 22:77-85 (1988)
©Martinus Nijhoff Publishers, Dordrecht - printed in the Netherlands.
Reprinted by permission of Kluwer Academic Publishers.

GREEK PHILOSOPHY AND THE ANTHROPOCENTRIC VISION

By Michael Soupios
Long Island University
C.W. Post Campus

Part I

When I first agreed to assess Greek attitudes toward nature and the environment, I assumed my investigations would lead rapidly to some important ecological wisdom that, *mutatis mutandis*, would be as salient to modern circumstance as it had been to the ancient world. In particular, I assumed that the great Hellenic ideals of symmetry, harmony, and balance would convey important insights regarding the proper and necessary relationships between man and nature.

I was mistaken. My examination of the ancient literature failed to yield any of the juicy apothegms I had anticipated. What I discovered instead was something that can only be termed, a "characteristic" lack of ecological interest, so much so that I am prepared to argue that the Greeks display a general philosophic indifference toward the natural environment. What has become a global concern for modern man appears not to have been a question for the Greeks.

13

The explanations for this lack of interest are complex and manifold but certainly a good portion of the answer lies with the enormous historical and technological distance separating our world from that of Plato's or Aristotle's. Clean air, acid rain, nuclear waste disposal, and natural resource management were hardly pressing issues in the fourth century B.C. But beyond the obvious, there are important reasons why the Greeks did not expend their philosophic energies on matters of this sort. In addition to not facing the urgent challenges of environmental pollution and dwindling natural resources, there was a powerful cultural idiom that mitigated against such orientations and, as I will attempt to demonstrate, it may be that this same cultural perspective contributed, at least in part, to today's ecological dilemma.

In order to proceed, it is first necessary to examine how the Greeks understood the term "nature" (*phusis*). Linguistically speaking, there are three distinct, though related, usages of the term *phusis*. One refers to the origin or genesis of a person or thing. A second meaning pertains to the material substrate out of which all things are made — the *arche* of the Milesian scientists. The final definition relates to the internal principle or structure of a thing. By the fourth century B.C., the third meaning appears to have become the dominant definition of *phusis* as illustrated by the frequency with which philosophers, sophists, playwrights, and poets employed this definition.[1]

One important conclusion that can be drawn from the linguistic evidence is the fact that the Greeks seem to have approached the concept of nature in a fundamentally different way than modern man. Specifically, the Greeks did not possess a holistic view of nature as the sum total of all things in time and space, i.e., nature as the entire physical universe, including plants, animals, and man.

The Ionian speculations of the sixth century B.C. approach this global view but fail to establish nature itself as the supra-category under which all forms of physical existence are logically subsumed. In short, the Greeks had nothing analogous to the modern notion of "Mother nature." The idea of nature as an all-wise and all-embracing force is a peculiarly modern concept traceable in part to the secularist reconstructions of the Enlightenment, where nature supplanted God as the providential force of the Universe[2] and to the poetic imagination of the Romantic Movement.

In contrast, the Greeks tended to view *phusis,* at least during the classical era, as something incomplete or unfinished. Nature, unaided, frequently lacked the wherewithal to achieve its own fruition and required the deliberate intervention of man — principally human *techne* in order to remedy its deficiencies. Nature seeks to endow its creatures with health but the healing hand of man is often needed to secure this end. Similarly, nature produces stone and marble but man alone hews these raw materials into fine art. Aristotle argues this point specifically in the *Politics,*[3] where he describes art and education as activities aimed expressly at correcting the shortcomings of nature. A related view is offered in a metaphorical context by Plato in the *Timaeus* where the voice of reason attempts to guide and correct the primordial, errant energies of the cosmos.[4]

These premises indicate some noteworthy things about how the Greeks perceived the relationship between man and *phusis.* More importantly, they suggest the singular significance man enjoyed in the Hellenic world view. A principal reason why the Greeks approached nature as they did is, in my view, intimately related to the fact that Hellenes made man the unassailable center of their cultural consciousness. As wide-ranging as Greek intellectual interests were, all speculations ultimately had a common focus-man himself. Werner Jaeger summarizes this point well in *Paideia:*[5]

> They (Hellenic cultural achievements) are the expressions of an anthropocentric attitude to life, which cannot be explained by or derived from anything else, and which pervades everything felt, made, or thought by the Greeks. Other nations made gods, kings, spirits: the Greeks made men.

The effects of this anthropocentric vision are evident from the very outset of Greek civilization. The turbulent tribal memories codified in the *Iliad* already reflect highly sophisticated attitudes about mankind. The chief Homeric message does not lie simply with the battlefields of Ilium but rather with the bittersweet path that stretches before all men and women; with the shared draught of glory and grief that ultimately unite an Achilles with a Priam.[6]

Perhaps the clearest illustration of Greek anthropocentrism is seen in the Hellenic religious outlook. Unlike the theomorphism of other ancient peoples, the Greeks fashioned their gods in their own image. In so doing,

15

they narrowed the distance between men and god to a degree later religious figures in the West found blasphemous.[7] The deities of the Olympian pantheon were conceived as elder brothers/sisters who inspired reverence but never servile fear. Given these attitudes, we can more fully appreciate the original meaning of the admonition, "know thyself." Long before the Delphian dictum bore philosophic relevance, it functioned as a religiously inspired prohibition for men to respect the boundary between things human and things divine. *Hubris* is a thoroughly logical crime in a cultural milieu that tended to apotheosize man. Though he was as Pindar said, "a creature of a day," man nevertheless was endowed with a special dignity the Greeks believed distinguished human life from all other forms of existence making man a first cousin to the gods themselves.

A further illustration of the anthropocentric lens by which the Hellenes saw life is reflected in the canons of Greek aesthetic theory. From earliest times, the Greek standard of beauty was almost exclusively human, more specifically, masculine. Greece is a land blessed with much natural beauty and certainly the Greeks were aware of the rustic grace of their native land. Still, the focus of Greek artistic endeavor fell squarely upon man himself. There is little in the surviving literature or art of the Greeks to indicate that they understood their ocean sunsets or mountain streams as comparable in beauty to the sleek, muscular lines of a well conditioned athlete.[8]

Plato, who spent considerable energy analyzing the psychology of beauty, offers some important insights in this regard. In the *Symposium,* where Diotima outlines the mysteries of eros, there is no mention whatsoever of natural beauty. All of the aesthetic categories mentioned — physical, spiritual, socio/political, scientific, noumenal — are all human related.[9]

Again, in the *Phaedrus* Plato makes clear his view that the "divine beauty" which sweeps over the lover; the beauty that nourishes the soul and allows it to grow wings and soar, is not the beauty of the natural world. It is instead a heavenly species of beauty mirrored in human form.[10]

The same dialogue also contains a rare bucolic episode in the life of Socrates that speaks directly to the human-centered values of Greek culture. Socrates and his young companion, Phaedrus, wander beyond the city gates in search of a suitable site to discuss a recent speech presented by the

16

celebrated rhetorician, Lysias. Socrates is struck by the beauty of his surroundings and describes at length his delight with the sweet sounds and sights of summer.[11] Phaedrus is surprised at Socrates' apparent unfamiliarity with these natural joys and asks whether Socrates ever ventures beyond the gates of Athens, to which Socrates responds:

> I must ask your forgiveness, my good friend. I am a lover of knowledge, and the men who dwell in the city are my teachers, and not the trees or the country.[12]

Subsequently, Socrates admits he has followed Phaedrus "like a hungry animal" only because of the book the young man has promised to share with him.

These same anthropocentric instincts may also have been relevant to the activities of the Milesian scientists. The movement from *mythos* to *logos* represented by the naturalistic speculations of thinkers such as Thales and Anaximander was almost certainly supported by the broad cultural conviction that man was a unique and separable entity from the rest of *phusis*. This assumption may have furnished the necessary theoretical distance that allowed the Greeks to interrogate nature in a revolutionary new way. The analytical spirit we find first among the Ionian Greeks implicitly asserts that man can stand apart from nature and examine its content and processes — that he alone can weigh, sift, measure, and explain the hidden logic of natural phenomena. This belief not only subsidized man's initial foray beyond the shadow world of religious belief, it also reinforced an already well established cultural premise, viz., that man was a notable and honorific exception to the rest of *phusis*.

Perhaps no other facet of Greek philosophy captures the essence of these anthropocentric convictions more fully than the teleological scheme that dominates so much of mature Hellenic thought.[13] The unequivocal focus of Greek teleology was the actualization of human potential — specifically the full attainment of man's capacities as a rational, moral, and spiritual being. This, the Greeks were convinced, was the key to *eudaemonia*; the fruition of human nature was at once the source of man's highest "good" and the guarantee of his greatest felicity. Toward the attainment of these human imperatives, the Greeks developed a value based calculus that tended to divide life into two broad categories, namely, the "means" and the "ends." Greek ethical theory, from the time of Socrates onward, never tires

17

of lamenting the frequency with which men squander their lives by inverting the proper relationship between the mere implements of life and life's higher purposes. The former enjoy significance only to the extent that they functionally support the attainment of the latter.

All of this has important bearing on how the Hellenes viewed the natural environment. The Greeks did not see man's teleological involvement as unique. They recognized a series of such relationships at various levels in nature. Aristotle argues, for instance, that plant life exists for the sake of herbivorous creatures. But as one might expect, he also reasons that man represents the pinnacle of all such associations. He is the final and ultimate link in a chain of teleological relationships and everything that lies below is subordinate to human need. It is in this spirit that Aristotle specifically identifies all plants and animal life as created for the express purpose of serving man.[14]

In essence then, Greek teleological belief, a natural by-product of Hellenic anthropocentrism, tended to deny, or at least obscure, nature's self-integrity. The environment enjoys no special sanctity of and in itself for the Greeks, but rather exists as a repository of raw materials designed to sustain man in his teleological journey. The governing logic here does not indicate much sentiment on behalf of symbiotic relation but suggests, instead, that man enjoys a special rank and privilege entitling him to access nature's gifts at his pleasure. In short, within the means/end equation, the Greeks clearly reduce nature to the level of means; and her bounty becomes part of the ordained right of man.

To sum up, the Greeks, placed man upon the altar in a way unlike any other ancient people. Their enthusiasm in this regard left an unmistakable stamp upon every facet of Hellenic civilization; art, religion, literature, science, philosophy, all bespeak a celebration of man at times bordering on auto-idolatry. This human centeredness did, of course deliver to Western man some of his most cherished and characteristic values. In the fullest sense, the Greeks must be credited with having lent original currency to the idea that man was an end in himself. Some of the West's most civilized and humane doctrines, including natural law theory and the concept of cosmopolis, share a common fount in Hellenic anthropocentrism.

Still, the analysis summons us to ask whether the Greeks did not also bestow a negative patrimony by arguing that man somehow stood beyond the scope of nature — a conceptual distinction that not only assumed humanity to be different from and superior to the rest of nature, but also alleged the unmitigated subservience of the natural environment to human need.

The English poet Shelly advises us that "We are all Greeks, our laws, our literature, our religion, our art..." If indeed, Greek culture was an architectonic force in the evolution of Western civilization, more, if it can be argued that the concept of Western culture itself is distinguishable from other sociocultural value systems by the very anthropocentrism we have described, then we must consider the real possibility that the rapacious acts of modern man toward the natural environment may represent a vestigial continuance of an ancient creed now equipped with unimagined technological potency.

Part II

While I am willing to argue, in broadest cultural terms, that the Greeks bear some culpability for today's questionable environmental practices, it is necessary to note certain countervailing Hellenic attitudes that clearly distinguish the ancient and modern world on this question. Aristotle tells us that the city-state was the final phase of a complex socio-political evolution. In his view, the polis satisfied all of the necessary criteria, material and otherwise, requisite for the good life.[15] By modern material standards, the city-state was a primitive affair at best. Aristotle's assertion, however, is not simply the product of technological naivete. It also reflects a level of material expectation substantively different than our own coupled with the philosophic conviction that there is little ultimate relationship between human happiness and material abundance. It is precisely this belief that has increasingly become an alien faith in the modern world. This modification in cultural attitude and its relevance to the major environmental issues of today will be considered next.

A fulcrum figure, linked to many of the changes I will suggest, was Francis Bacon. In great measure, Bacon helped articulate a radical new ethos regarding man's relationship to nature, and perhaps most significantly, assisted in redefining the meaning of the "good life."

Bacon was a revolutionary thinker in at least three respects. First and foremost, he was the apostle of a new scientific method aimed at dislodging

19

the ancient tyranny of Aristotle, who, in Bacon's opinion, had corrupted natural philosophy by attempting to fashion the world out of categories.[16] Bacon demanded a decisive break with all such "idols of the theatre,"[17] that is, the received systems of earlier philosophers. In particular, his proposed "Great Instauration" sought to replace syllogistic reasoning and the quest for philosophic first causes, with an experimentally based system of operative physics. Methodologically speaking, Bacon can legitimately be credited with having lent a bold new trajectory to Western science.[18]

In his zeal to reform scientific method, Bacon also prescribed a new definition of philosophy itself. His position centers around what he saw as an essential need for philosophic endeavor to bear "fruit" — one of Bacon's most frequently employed images. In the *Novum Organum*, he announces that:

> Wherefore as in religion we are warned to show our faith by works, so in philosophy by the same rule the system should be judged by its fruits, and pronounced frivolous if it is barren of grape and olive...[19]

Later in the same work, Bacon characterizes the philosophers of old as spiders, i.e., aimless web spinners. The new paradigm advocated by Bacon is that of the bee — industrious and active — because "this is the true business of philosophy."[20]   Ancient speculation is specifically condemned as otiose — "fruitful of controversies but barren of works".[21] More generally, Bacon repudiates the *bios theoretikos* or contemplative life that the Greeks saw as the highest human virtue and the activity most consistent with the natural ends of the rational animal.[22]

Bacon's new philosopher is, in short, the new scientist; someone capable of endowing man with material benefits. Implicit in this redefinition is the stripping away of philosophy's traditional centers of interest. Bacon is little concerned with matters of ethical value, conscience, will, or obligation. Issues of "worth" are displaced by issues of "use" and, as a result, a new question emerges on the philosophic horizon. No longer would Bacon have us inquire, "Am I a good man?". He proposes instead that we ask, "Am I a materially comfortable man?".

This new question in turn points to the third revolutionary element in Bacon's thought. It concerns a fundamental alteration of value ascription.

For the ancient Greeks, authentic human existence mandated the attainment of intellectual and moral excellence. A modicum of material prosperity was necessary, as Aristotle tells us, but these external goods were devoid of intrinsic value and assumed a relative worth only when dedicated to larger purpose.[23] It is instructive to compare the Hellenic recipe for happiness with the neo-eudaemonism of Bacon. "We must not think," says Aristotle,

> that the man who is to be happy will need many things or great things, merely because he cannot be supremely happy without external goods; for self-sufficiency and action do not involve excess, and we can do noble acts without ruling earth and sea, for even with moderate advantages one can act virtuously, and it is enough that we should have so much as that; for the life of the man who is active in accordance with virtue will be happy.[24]

In contrast, Bacon defines happiness exclusively in terms of material and utilitarian procurement. The good life is the life of plenty. Bacon's gauge here is thoroughly unrelated to rational and moral precept, but relies instead upon the degree of largesse gained through *experimenta fruictifera* (experiments of fruit). The Hellenic admonition concerning the inversion of means and ends is explicitly discarded by Bacon. Indeed, his entire program is nothing less than a concrete effort to install means as ends. The "external goods" to which Aristotle assigned secondary significance become for Bacon the *summum bonum*.

All of these material commodities will issue from a single source according to Bacon. Nature, analyzed and manipulated by the new scientific method, will succor mankind in ways never before dreamed. In a real sense, Bacon views nature as a cornucopia ready to be seized and emptied. The mentality here, is clearly aggressive and exploitive. Bacon's ideal is to "command nature in action",[25] to increasingly place more and more of nature "under constraint." The scientific community, the Solomon's House of Bacon's *New Atlantis,* will organize and lead the expeditions against nature — its ultimate objective being the achievement of a situation "When by art and the hand of man she (nature) is forced out of her natural state, and squeezed and molded."[26] The Greeks were the first to interrogate nature but they did so chiefly as an intellectual exercise. Bacon proposes an inquisition in the spirit of utilitarian onslaught.

21

In closing, I wish to state for the record that I am very much a creature of the times and I would be the last to surrender the many Baconian "fruits" to which I have become so thoroughly accustomed. Still, it is crucial that even as we accept the gifts of Bacon's formula, we recognize the need to define his famous aspiration, viz, "relief of the human estate," in a comprehensive manner. Both Bacon and the Greeks salute the sovereign efficacy of reason but they dedicate man's rational energies to radically different ends. By offering a materialistically inspired definition of "relief", Bacon not only contributed in some sense to the callous disregard of nature and her resources, he also helped deflect modern man away from his necessary involvement with larger philosophic concerns. In itself, material abundance is but a pale aspect of human happiness. The life worth living, perforce, addresses issues of value, morality, justice, and beauty. The fully human existence, in brief, dedicates itself to the acquisition of wisdom — something distinct from technological cunning. There is little in Bacon that recommends this course, despite the fact that such an attainment indeed, constitute the supreme "relief of the human estate."

NOTES

[1]See F.E. Peters, *Greek Philosophical Terms - Historical Lexicon*: New York: New York University Press, 1967 p. 158 and J.W. Beardslee Jr., *The Use of Phusis in 5th Century Greek Literature*, Chicago, University of Chicago Press, 1918, pp 2-3.

[2]See D. Marnet, *French Thought in the Eighteenth Century*, trans. L. M. Levin, New York: Prentice Hall Inc. 1929, esp. p. 43; and P. Hazard, *European Thought in the Eighteenth Century*, New Haven: Yale University Press, 1954, p. 113.

[3]*Politics* 7.1337a15, *Physics* 2.199a8.15-19, *Nicomachean Ethics* 7.1140a4.10-17.

[4]*Timaeus* 48 a-b

[5]Werner Jaeger, *Paideia*, vol.I. New York: Oxford University Press, 1945, p xxiii.

[6]See *Iliad*, Book 24.

[7]St. Augustine finds these tendencies appalling and he condemns them aggressively in his *Confessions* (4.15, 7.20-21, 13.21).

[8]Even when the Greeks do comment upon natural beauty, it is frequently within the context of some larger observation about man. In the *Greek Anthology* the following lines are found, but they in fact refer to the pitifully ephemeral nature of man: "Pleasant are the fair things of nature — earth, sea, stars, the orbs of moon and sun. All else in fearfulness and pain." For a discussion of this part see Butcher, *Some Aspects of the Greek Genius*, p. 162.

[9]*Symposium* 210 A-

[10]*Phaedrus*, 0251 a-c.

[11]*Ibid.*, B-D.

[12]*Ibid*, 230 D.

23

[13]An exception here being the Epicureans.

[14]*Politics* 1.1256 b12.

[15]*Ibid.*, 1.1252 b8-9.

[16]Francis Bacon, *The New Organon*, LXIII.

[17]*Ibid*, XXIX-XLIV.

[18]One important element missing from Bacon's new method is the formal use of hypothesis.

[19]*New Organon* LXXIII

[20]*Ibid.*, XCV.

[21]Francis Bacon, *The Great Instauration* in *The New Organon and Related Writings*. ed. F. H. Anderson, New York: Liberal Arts Press, 1960, p. 8.

[22]See Aristotle's *Nicomachean Ethics*, especially Book 10, Chap. 7.

[23]See *Politics* 7.1325b4-5.

[24]*Nicomachean Ethics* 10.1179a8.

[25]Bacon, *Great Instauration*, p. 19.

[26]*Ibid.*, p. 25.

HUMAN BEING AND NATURAL WORLD
Commentary on Shirk and Soupios

By Arnold Berleant
Long Island University
C.W. Post Campus

In her rich and impassioned plea for an environmental ethics, Evelyn Shirk has surveyed the ground on which environmental ethics must stand. It is her main claim that this new direction of ethical thought differs thoroughly from past ethics and thus requires a new kind of ethical thinking and new kinds of solutions to ethical problems. Until now it was easy to adopt the self-indulgent view that nature was out there, a stable and permanent field from which we could freely harvest what we had not sowed, a benefit which incurred no obligations or responsibilities. This comfortable myth has changed, as we are now forced to recognize, and we find that, if we wish not only to live well and happily but merely to survive, we cannot continue to act in narrow ignorance, selfishly, and without reciprocation.

How have we come to this pass? Whatever the material and social causes of the practice of appropriating the natural world, we human animals find it necessary to construct explanations that justify that practice, and ethics has a long tradition of apologetic, of justifying what we want to do in the name of rights. Both Evelyn Shirk and Michael Soupios have done important work investigating the philosophic origins of our common beliefs and reasons.

Shirk finds that ethics in the past has concerned itself only with the private matter of individual well being. Further, she identifies in the hallowed dualism of mind and body the basis for our conviction that nature consists of our physical surroundings, separate and apart from the spiritual realm of thought and meaning that we take as the special human province. Nature is the source of our nurture, to be sure, but it is a realm outside. Soupios, on his part, sees in the anthropomorphism of classical Greek civilization an attitude that regards nature as raw material for man to order and to dominate. And he finds in the anthropocentrism of Greek thought the origin of the conception that the world is to be understood and judged by human standards of beauty and of good. While nature is an harmonious order, it is a qualitative order and man stands at the apex of the hierarchy. Moreover, when this attitude was replaced at the beginning of the modern scientific era with a mechanistic model of nature by such people as Francis Bacon, we divided ourselves from nature in order to conquer it.

I am not sure Shirk is quite correct in her characterization of earlier ethical thought and practice as concerned with the fitness of the individual soul. This was certainly the case with the medieval Christian tradition and it has continued in pervasive social form from the Protestant Reformation to the present day. Yet it would be mistaken, I think, to export our indelible individualism to the fourth century B.C., for the evidence in the writings of Plato certainly attests to the correspondence if not the identity of individual and social good, and in Aristotle to a conception of human good as rooted in the social order.

But these ideas are not our own, and here Soupios reminds us further of the classical Greeks' beliefs about humans and nature, where people must complete the unfinished matter of nature by introducing an order into it. That this order turns out to be modeled on human goals and human good is no coincidence. Moreover, while Bacon represents a major shift away from this anthropomorphic conception of nature, it is to an understanding of nature as something separate and apart, a foreign and different place and thus a fitting object for people to dominate and use.

I would read the history of Greek philosophy somewhat differently from Soupios by seeing in Greek thinking a greater sense of similarity and harmony between human beings and the natural world. All things in the world, people, plants, animals, even inorganic objects, have their characteristic motion, a force which presses them toward the fulfillment of

26

the potentialities inherent in their nature. In this fashion they strive to complete their natural cycles within the order of a rational universe and so achieve their proper end or entelechy. Where Soupios is entirely correct is in identifying that rational order as thoroughly anthropomorphic, conceived on the model of humans striving after goals. Moreover that order of nature places rational man at its pinnacle as both the model and beneficiary of the whole process. There is a harmony of similars here, then, but it is a harmony that reflects and serves the human ideal.

Whatever the truth about philosophic origins, there is no debate on the need for developing ideas that reflect our present understanding of human beings and of nature and of the good of both. Shirk is clearly right in stating that environmental ethics is group ethics, and insofar as people can use intelligence to guide their behavior in the natural and social conditions under which we must live, the Greek example may be of use. We realize, as the Greeks did before, that people are implicated together in a single moral web, but unlike them we now know that it is a web that includes the natural world as well as ourselves. In fact, nothing so needs re-thinking as does our conception of what that natural world is. Here Shirk and I share the idea that we can no longer safely worship before the false idol of the marketplace ["words hastily abstracted from things"] that sees nature as separate and apart from ourselves, something out there to be tamed, shaped, and used. For thinking and acting in this way is at no one's expense but our own. We suffer from the disorders of a nature which we ourselves have created. Indeed, it is we alone who suffer (along with other sentient creatures), for nature is really the ethically neutral universe in which all processes and events will continue mindlessly under conditions of overwhelmingly toxic air and water, inescapable radiation, sterility, and barrenness. It is just we who will no longer be present, and it is only we who will suffer the loss, or would have were we around to suffer.

These conditions, then, do require new ideas, and about what it is to be human as well as about what we understand by nature. These conditions require more than anything the recognition that the two — human being and natural world — cannot be kept apart or understood as if they were separate. People and nature are inseparable, both aspects of the same continuous processive order and both shaped by that same process. Perhaps we should introduce Spinoza into this philosophical search, for he more than anyone recognized the continuity and harmony of humans with the

27

world order. We are all threads of the same cloth, but whether it be our wedding gown or shroud is for us to decide.

PROPERTY RIGHTS AND THE ENVIRONMENT

By Christopher P. Mooney
Nassau Community College

Despite the large consensus on the need to develop an environmental ethic which addresses the huge problems and deep conflicts of interest involved in the use and control of the natural resources of the earth, there is little agreement about which practical measures will best resolve these issues that face mankind as we enter the twenty-first century. This situation is not too surprising since longstanding fundamental concepts and powerful vested interests are involved. As with so many moral problems, our legal concepts and traditions need thorough rexamination and readjustment. In particular, the whole concept of property rights and especially property rights in land require careful scrutiny.[1] It will be the purpose of this paper to begin to examine this long neglected topic in relation to the crisis in the environment.

It would be impossible here, of course, to treat adequately or authoritatively all the problems involved in the ownership of land, but some suggestions can be made which might fruitfully advance the cause of a better system of environmental responsibility. Nor do we have the time to trace the evolution of present day policies and principles governing the ownership of land, but it is certainly clear that Western societies have one of the most elaborate systems of property rights in land and that they are at the root of much of the difficulty. On the other hand, recently much ink has been spilt on the life and customs of Precolumbian Americans, but even if the most flattering pictures were true, we could not return to such a way of life if we tried, and thus little attention will be given to comparisons with them.[2]

There is hope, however, that some of the insights and values of thinkers such as Thoreau and Aldo Leopold might be made part of a new way of seeing and treating the environment and, perhaps, incorporated into a less hazardous environmental ethic.[3] What needs to be appreciated, of course, is that such an ethic must be beneficial to all, not just pleasing to a small number of naturalists who live in the countryside. Indeed, it cannot be emphasized enough that property rights stand at the center of every issue we face regarding the environment both for city and country folk.

Since land is the basis for access to the environment, property rights in land necessarily affect environmental issues. Broadly speaking, the environment consists of all the influences-cultural, political, social, as well as physical - that surround human society. But for present purposes, we must limit our discussion to laws governing the geophysical aspects of environmental concern. And land is the most important domain of the ecosystem. Access to land provides the only sure way in which we may interact with all aspects of the environment. For better or worse, those who hold property rights to land will affect and be affected by the environment.[4] Moreover, the distinct advantages that different parcels of land enjoy are often as important as the size of the holdings and their value is most often directly related to environmental factors. Even when they are directly related, they are indirectly related, for urban land must also have specific physical features in order to support a large population. Everyone knows that Manhattan is built on granite bedrock, is located in a good harbor, has a moderate climate, enjoys access to adequate water supplies, and is surrounded by good farmland. It is really not too difficult to understand then, just on the basis of these environmental factors, why New York City has become the preeminent city in the United States. To be sure, people can destroy, and presently seem bent on doing so, those advantages, but they are there by nature, not because of man's efforts.

This is why we are concerned with the question of environmental ethics in relation to ownership of land. As has been said already, while there has been some recent work and several good suggestions on different

30

aspects of environmental ethics and property rights, it still remains an area much neglected in law and philosophy.[5] Indeed, it seems that only a few voices have been raised in defense of the environment within the professional legal community. Things are improving, but not rapidly enough for it is harder to rebuild valuable things than to neglect or destroy them, unfortunately.

A number of people, in fact, have remarked that the present generation seems bent upon proving that it is within its power to leave the earth a barren, uninhabitable place even without the outbreak of nuclear warfare. So voraciously do we devour the earth and its treasures that within the not-too-distant future extreme scarcity of primary resources will be a fundamental problem. Even now forests are being defoliated, soil is being eroded, seas are being fished out, yet the general response is much lamentation, pointed accusations and direful predictions, but very little in the way of resourceful restrictions or regulations. Part of the problem can be traced to the lack of legal jurisdiction both on a national and on an international scale, but much of it comes from the difficulty of overcoming the inertia created by the tremendous speed in which the huge industrial world has been moving against the fragile ecosystem of this lovely planet.

The situation has almost become criminal in the United States. To cite one comment, almost at random:

No other country in the history of the world has devoured inorganic resources so voraciously and developed an economy which seems so dependent on the continuous enlargement of its own appetite. It is difficult to view the present trends and the continuing expectations of the large urban populations of this wealthy country with anything but alarm.[6]

When something like 6 percent of the world's population consumes close to 30 percent of the world's resources, there is grave cause for alarm. If others were to imitate the American lifestyle(and, of course, they are bring encouraged to do so), there is not much chance that the planet could sustain such a form of consumerism for more than a score of years or more.

The most important point that needs repeating is simply that the world is a place of finite resources, of diminishing returns. Even with the

31

most efficient utilization of the earth and its fruits, we live in a time when conservation is an economic, as well as an ethical, imperative. And time is fast running out. It is worth remembering, in addition, that environmental protection and conservation is not a new topic in the American political agenda.[7] While in the first half of the twentieth century it suffered neglect, and even scorn, in the big bucks, big business atmosphere of those days, concern for the environment can be traced back to Jefferson and down to Theodore Roosevelt at least. Consider the contemporaneous sound of this Declaration from a Conference of United States Governors prepared in 1880:

> We agree that the land should be so used that erosion and soil wash shall cease; and that there should be reclamation of arid and semi-arid regions by means of irrigation, and of swamp and overflowed regions by means of drainage; that the waters should be so conserved and used as to promote navigation, to enable the arid regions to be reclaimed by irrigation, and to develop power in the interests of the people; that the forests which regulate our rivers, support our industries, and promote the fertility and productiveness of the soil should be preserved and perpetuated; that the minerals found so abundantly beneath the surface should be so used as to prolong their utility; that the beauty, healthfulness, and habitability of our country should be preserved and increased; that sources of national wealth exist for the benefit of the people, and that monopoly thereof should not be tolerated.[8]

What went wrong? Clearly much of the problem can be traced to the lack of carefully monitored land use regulations. And this, of course, can be at least partially blamed upon an ill-conceived conception of property rights in land. What we need to do is see whether or not we can outline a reasonable and environmentally sound notion of property rights that will reflect both economic and ethical requirements.

Immediately we are confronted with several obstacles: (1) entrenched attitudes toward property rights; (2) competing conceptions of economic efficiency; (3) fundamental disagreements about what responsibility is owed to future generations;and (4) the problem of "social costs." We shall give our attention to each of these in turn.

32

(1) Entrenched Attitudes Toward Property Rights

Anyone who has been slightly awake for the past few decades knows that the clamor for "rights" fills the halls of our political institutions and is on the lips of every constituent lobby group.[9] Yet little has been said of late about "duties" or "responsibilities." People seem to imagine that rights come first, last and always. In fact, they are really secondary factors in a just political and legal system for, while important, human duties are more fundamental. Simone Weil said it best:

> The notion of obligations comes before that of rights, which is subordinate and relative to the former. A right is not effectual by itself, but only in relation to the obligation to which it corresponds, the effective exercise of a right springing not from the individual who possesses it, but from other men who consider themselves as being under a certain obligation toward him. Recognition of an obligation makes it effectual. An obligation which goes unrecognized by anyone loses none of the full force of its existence. A right which goes unrecognized by anyone is not worth very much.[10]

This point is especially true when we consider property rights in land, for since the control of land gives an individual or corporation power over the whole environment that the parcel comes in contact with, there is a tremendous responsibility to utilize those ownership rights reasonably. Thus we find that more and more government units are enacting land use controls over property for environmental reasons. The pollution, defoliation or outright destruction of land through manufacturing, lumbering or mining the earth have consequences that require careful regulation and monitoring. And even mere usage such as with driving an automobile creates environmental problems which can be considerable.

These facts are especially significant when we consider that land ownership is a unique property right. No parcel of land is exactly like any other. And none can be moved around. The Dutch try but, except for some small portion of the surface, they are unsuccessful. Nature is so constructed as to make it impossible to create more land. It is a finite resource and all it contains can never be expanded. It can be efficiently utilized, of course, and it can be wasted, as all-too-often is the case. What is needed is a system of property rights which encourages maximum utilization of land

33

and its resources. Property rights which give absolute control of land will not do that, and hence need to be reconsidered and rewritten. Recognition of this lies at the core of much work being done by environmental philosophers, lawyers and activists.[11]

As with all legal rights, public awareness comes from experience. The strict enforcement of rights and duties makes people conscious of their prerogatives and responsibilities better than abstract discussions or philosophical debates. So long as the courts ground their decisions upon reasonable premises, they need not worry about public reaction. To see this we need only witness the changes wrought in the area of civil rights in the last twenty-five years. Of course, in a democracy, there is always the problem of minority versus majority rights, but when the issue of property and the environment is objectively considered, it is hard to see how anyone can rationally oppose greater vigilence in enforcing environmental controls.[12]

Therefore, private property rights need not, indeed should not, be absolute. They are just as open to regulation and limitation as any other form of rights when they conflict with other rights. Moreover, the traditional arguments for property in land fail to adequately demonstrate the reasonableness or necessity of transferring what is a common heritage of all mankind into the hands of a few individuals or major corporations. Even those who urge the private distribution of land titles, do so with an awareness of the need for careful stewardship on the part of owners. The right to "destroy" one's property may apply to chattel, but it cannot apply to land. Unfortunately, though there is an increasing awareness of the permanence of some forms of pollution and environmental damage, the right to use land in whatever fashion the owner deems desirable is still widely professed. Especially when it has been argued that a particular use would be economically beneficial to the owner, prohibition of such use has been rare or coupled with compensation. The constitutional provision against "takings" as found in the Fifth and Fourteenth Amendments has often been interpreted in a manner detrimental to the public interest and unjustified in terms of individual rights.[13] Sometimes there are greater responsiblities of the law than seeing that every owner of land can reap as much profit from his site without worrying about the long term consequences to society as a whole.

But, if there is constitutional protection against unjust "takings", there is also constitutional provision for regulation of land use. The difficulty arises in judging when a regulation becomes a "taking" and when it is the rightful exercise of the police power of the state.[14] Since, in its regulation of land use, the state is not liable for compensation, it is very important to the individual property owner and to society itself who shall bear the burden of the "social costs." We shall deal with this issue below; however, there must be no doubt about the reasonableness of balancing public and private interests in the use of land. Moreover, it must be recognized that to date the tendency has been to give the benefit to the private party and place the burden on the public. To quote Paul W. Gates, one of the outstanding historians of American land policy:

> While the management of our remaining public domain is still a most serious and important problem, the management of that portion of our territory that has become private property is a more serious problem. In fact, the old distinction between public and private property is losing its sharpness, or is being eroded away, and for the sake of later generations it should be. Has a man a right to destroy good irreplaceable agricultural land by covering it up with cement or by strip-mining it? Can a man do what is most profitable for him with his own? But is it his own in an unlimited sense? Rather has he not received from society a bundle of rights which society protects but which society may also limit or modify or even take over? Is not the public land that has passed into private hands a trust? Older and more crowded societies than ours have long since been obligated to take this stand, and we should come to this point of view also and soon.[15]

What is definitely needed is clear, unambiguous promulgation of the rights and duties necessary for the just distribution of property in land. Included in the statement must be prohibitions against environmentally unsound exploitation of the earth and its resources. This will have to cover both the issues of conservation and pollution. We should remember that, varying Lord Acton's more famous maxim — Power corrupts, and absolute power corrupts absolutely — power pollutes, and unregulated power pollutes permanently. Property rights are a species of power; unregulated property rights both corrupt and pollute.

(2) Competing Conceptions of Economic Efficiency

It would be equally impossible to examine the different conceptions of economic efficiency that are current in either academia or the business world, but once again we will content ourselves with a few words on this issue, since it's importance cannot be overlooked or denied. Much of the debate surrounding environmental issues and ethics involves contrasting views as to what constitutes economic efficiency. If, as has been insisted, there is both an ethical and an economic motive for the maximum utilization of natural resources, there must be some agreed upon standard whereby we may measure such utilization. The problem is much more subtle than the competing systems of market-based versus command-based economics. Efficiency in economics cannot be determined with a simple formula as it can in thermodynamics.[16]

It must be recognized that social utility is not always advanced by increased productivity or greater efficiency which are measured by purely economic indicators. There is more to economic efficiency than mere cost per unit, especially when one considers the huge social and environment costs that most large scale manufacturing or mining industries entail. If we have learned anything at all from the industrial revolution, we have learned that the hidden costs of an otherwise "harmless" activity can be enormous. One does not have to accept the Marxist analysis of alienation nor the concept of "surplus value" to acknowledge that much so-called efficiency is very counterproductive, at least in human and environmental terms.

What we need is an economics of scale.[17] After all, we must keep in mind that human beings are middle-sized creatures. They are neither too little nor too big for the environment. Hence, moderate means and moderate ends are as economically sensible as they are ethically commendable. John Ruskin was not being sentimental or unrealistic when he wrote:

> A nation which desires true wealth, desires it moderately, and can, therefore, distribute it with kindness, and possess it with pleasure; but one which desires false wealth, desires it immoderately, and can neither dispense it with justice, nor enjoy it in peace.[18]

There are those who think the problem is big business, and there are those who are equally convinced that it is big government. Unfortunately, neither group tends to see that the true common enemy is bigness itself.

36

Both misunderstand the real role of scale in economic and social efficiency. Everything must be kept in proportion to its function, otherwise waste and/or inefficiency creep into the system. And nature herself is a very intricate system in which tiny mistakes can cause huge disasters. The only way in which we can combat pollution and further conservation is through moderate means and careful allocation of resources. This means that property rights must be checked by social and environmental obligations. For some this will seem like a direct limitation being imposed upon their right to accumulate property, but in fact it is only the minimum necessary means whereby the social whole can look after its interests, most especially the conservation of human life and the natural resources of the earth.

This does not mean that private property rights need to be eliminated or that the free market economy shall be by-passed in favor of a socially orchestrated regime. And we shall address the problem of social costs below, but at the moment it is worth remembering that the technique of using the market to determine the proper price for all commodities or maximum efficiency is both pernicious and counterproductive. It is pernicious because not all values can be given quantitative rankings, and it is counterproductive because it may actually lead one to emphasize factors which actually are relatively minor in importance.

Mark Sagoff has written forcefully and clearly about such a narrow approach:

Cost-benefit analysis becomes a ludicrous exercise when it extends the concept of a market failure, in this way, to include mistakes, shortcomings, and idiocies of all kinds. We do not use markets to determine the number of planets. Why should we devise markets, then, to establish whether an environmental policy makes cultural, aesthetic, or moral sense? People have ideas; they have beliefs they can defend; they have arguments to offer concerning the right and wrong way to treat wilderness, wildlife, rivers and lakes. How can surrogate markets, however ingenious, determine whether these beliefs are true or whether these arguments are sound? Markets provide a forum for the exchange of commodities not the exchange of ideas. To use market analysis is not to find a neutral way to choose among values but to insist upon efficiency, that is, a particular value. It is to respect only one set of opinions- those put forward by certain economists and to provide a shadow price to all the rest.[19]

What he is emphasizing is that no purely economic notion of efficiency exists since there is no purely economic activity. The ideal market just does not exist, nor will it ever. Furthermore, as economic activities become more and more intertwined through the development of international markets and corporations different aspects of production and exchange will take on different values. Time in one society will not be as precious as in another, and so forth.

Finally, we should also stress that growth has its limits and that we live in a finite world. No resource is unlimited, not even sunlight. Belief that there are no limits to human endeavors has led to tragedy since the days of the ancient Greeks. In fact, the Delphic maxim, "Know Thyself," was often viewed as a reminder that man is not a god, and must always take into account the human dimensions of our activities. Otherwise, we shall fall prey to our own arrogance.

(3) Man's Responsibility To Future Generations

As great as the environmental problems of the present world population are, the impact of current environmental practices upon the future generations of mankind is even more critical. It is essential to remember that the terms "mankind" or "human race" include, at once, every person that is, has been, and is yet to be. That is a huge number, but more importantly it is a sum which reminds us of our direct connection with previous generations and our immense responsibility for future ones. Some might immediately counter with the argument that non-existent persons have no rights and hence we have no obligations toward them. But this is too facile, for the future generation of mankind is now being born. One generation is of necessity continuous with the next. Unless we were to halt reproduction immediately and universally, we cannot avoid considering those who will undoubtedly inherit the earth.

The question is, then, what is owed to our offspring?[20] How much of the resources of the earth must we conserve for them? Obviously, since they are all finite in extent, we cannot give them more, or even the same amount, than we enjoy. It must be somewhat less, somewhat diminished. The hard choices come in determining how much less and in which areas.

38

Fortunately, we cannot diminish the land space itself. That remains constant as we have already noted, but it is entirely possible that certain portions of the globe could be made uninhabitable, just as some have recently been made inhabitable. And it does seem that a primary responsibility is to conserve, at the very least, the present inhabitable space upon which mankind may live. We have seen again and again that rapid exploitation or poorly conceived development of the surface of the earth will have more far reaching effects than practically any other form of environmental disaster with the possible exception of nuclear war or accident. Cutting down the trees of the rain forest in the Amazon is as great a disaster as Chernobyl.

Directly allied to this are the issues of air and water pollution. They are as equally detrimental to future generations as soil or mineral depletion. The burning of Kuwait is clear evidence to any skeptic. In addition, it is clear that they are — especially in the present levels practiced in most industrial nations—unnecessary. It is simply not essential for a reasonable standard of living to emit hydrocarbons into the atmosphere or dump toxic wastes into the waterways in the quantities currently allowed. Even the most ancient rules of the common law forbid creating a nuisance through sights, sounds, smells, or other means. We must make sure that there is stringent enforcement of laws governing all types of pollution and disturbance of the quiet enjoyment of land. Nature deserves at least that much respect. We owe it, moreover, to our children and grandchildren.

More difficult problems and more technical issues arise when we turn to the area of actual conservation. Pollution in the strong meaning of the term is simply not acceptable.[21] Some things may simply run out before we can find alternatives. Yet this cannot justify a selfish consumption on the part of everyone now. Indeed it would seem to imply the careful conservation of all limited or scarce natural resources. It is striking to think that while nuclear energy had not been dreamt of one hundred years ago, people were under the assumption that oil and coal deposits were in a real sense being newly created under the earth. And now we know that both nuclear energy and fossil fuels involve very hazardous health and environmental dangers. In other words, while new sources of energy may be hidden from us now, presently imagined possibilities may equally be illusory. We cannot be too prudent.

Thomas Jefferson was one who took his responsibility toward future generations quite seriously. In a long letter from Paris to James Madison he laid out his ideas regarding the sweeping social and political reforms necessary to give every man his due. "The question, whether one generation of men has a right to bind another, seems never to have been started on this or our side of the water," he wrote. "Yet it is a question of such consequences as not only to merit decision, but also to place among the fundamental principles of every government." Then Jefferson set down this basic principle: "that the earth belongs in usufruct to the living: that the dead have neither powers nor rights over it."[22] Utilizing Buffon's mortality tables that each generation was expected to live approximately 19 years during its time of majority, he applied his principles to three areas. First, regarding landed property, every generation had the right to labor the earth. No one should be able to deny another man his right to employment by extensive holdings in land which excluded new members of the human race through exclusive property rights. This was a notion he apparently owed to Locke. Second, regarding public debt, every generation should pay its own way. One generation should not be allowed to burden the next with its profligacy. Could there be a more relevent topic today with the enormous deficits that the young are going to have to pay off? Third, regarding the rule of law, he argued that each generation should have the right to establish its own constitution, for that right would free men from the agreements or contracts of the past in which they had no part. Those who argue that we must only interpret the Constitution in the light of "original intent" of the Founders should take note of this point especially.

Unfortunately, we are not able to explore these ideas of Jefferson in any detail: but we must note that he wishes to give every generation the chance to fashion its own future, and at the same time he reminds us of the need to consider those to come (for theoretically every generation will have descendants). Thus, we have an obligation not to exploit or waste what is given lest future generations are harmed.

(4) The Problem Of Social Costs

With the problem of social costs our discussion could become more technical, for there are many aspects of this issue that require detailed facts and figures. However, without being too superficial, we can consider the question broadly. Also, it is obviously a question that is related to the problem of competing notions of economic efficiency which we addressed above.

Ronald Coase outlined this problem, and indeed he gave it its title, in an essay published just three decades ago.[23] However, it is something which economists have been dealing with, albeit somewhat unwittingly, for a long time. The issue centers on how to deal effectively and economically with the side-effects of production, especially those which are disturbing, harmful, or polluting. Basically, there are two ways of countering these side-effects and limiting their influence upon society as a whole. First, there is the possibility of government regulation. Through fines, restrictions and/or taxes an industry might be forced to pay for the harmful effects of its productivity. Second, there is the traditional pricing mechanism conditioned by the legal liability of the manufacturer to pay for damages caused by his activities. It is the second approach that Coase supports, for he believes that the market place price mechanism by-passes unnecessary, inefficient, bureaucratic elements but still arrives at desired results.

Insofar as Coase's solution would eliminate the need for bureaucratic structures to police the environment, there can be no faulting his position. As in metaphysics, so also in politics, there is no need to multiply entities beyond necessity. We must always endeavor to keep things, and most importantly institutions, simple. But this requires careful consideration of rights and responsibilities. Property owners are not likely to restrain themselves voluntarily, if there is an opportunity for greater benefit to themselves or their interests, when they act selfishly and shortsightedly. Hence, the problem of social costs becomes a problem of legal liability. E.J. Mishan has understood this well. He wrote:

> The competitive market has long been recognized by economists as an inexpensive mechanism for allocating goods and services with tolerable efficiency. Once it is observed that the production of 'bads', or noxious spillover effects, have begun, increasingly, to accompany the production of goods, one might be excused for talking about a serious failure of the market mechanism. *In fact the failure is not to be attributed to the market itself, but to the legal framework within which it operates. In particular, we must remind ourselves that what constitutes a cost to commercial enterprise depends upon the existing law.* If the law recognized slavery the costs of labour would be no greater than the costs involved in capturing a man and maintaining him thereafter at subsistence level.[24] (emphasis added)

Hence, we are brought back to the old problem of property rights and their restrictions. If the state licenses a corporation to operate a radio or television network, it clearly creates vested interests, both on the part of the corporation and on the part of the state. Generally speaking, so long as those interests are met satisfactorily, each party goes its own way and enjoys the benefits derived from its particular interest. But once either party feels that it is not receiving sufficient reward for its contribution, trouble begins. If the dissatisfaction comes from the state, the corporation is likely to contest the complaint and argue in favor of "free enterprise" or "freedom of the press." But that very same corporation is more than likely, in fact it is almost certainly, going to introduce proceedings if it feels that its privileges have been infringed upon by any other party. Of course, it will cite its license and the prerogatives that it entails, and it will proclaim its public-minded spirit, and finally it will talk about its investment of capital, creativity and sheer hard work in building its reputation. What it will undoubtedly fail to mention is the fact that its very existence is owed neither to the state nor to its many contributions, but ultimately to the existence of the electromagnetic spectrum. Without that fundamental fact of nature, there could be no radio or television. In the same way, rights to property in land are the result of the existence, and importance, of land. If environmental factors force society to make utilization of land more expensive, then so be it. The social cost is not such a problem after all. Only when owners can pass along the costs of production to the public and do not have to learn to operate in a cleaner and more conservatively conscious manner, does it become a serious issue.

In an extremely influential article Garrett Hardin outlined what he termed "The Tragedy of the Commons."[25] Basically the thesis of his essay was that since every man will seek to maximize his gain and minimize his loss when engaging in economic activity, communally owned property will be over-grazed, or over-fished, since the individual will not have to pay the expenses for his exploitation alone but rather in common with all the others using the property. Therefore, the tendency will be to try to extract as much production for as little cost as possible. As a consequence, the commons will be overutilized quickly. Only by allocating specific portions of the commons to private parties will each party attempt to conserve and protect the property entrusted to him. Hardin argues that private property is the only way in which to protect the environment from being completely depleted or ruined, since the private owner will have to pay for all the costs that are incurred in production, since there is no one else to shift the burden upon.

Combined with Coase's ideas, Hardin's make sense; however, both men leave out one vital factor. Neither the commons nor any other site is independent. Even an island is surrounded by the sea. We are all on this earth together and, if we do not all take greater responsibility for the environment, everyone will suffer. That much should be clear in the smog that obscures our vision and clogs our breathing.

In conclusion, it is fair to say that only if property rights are so construed that maintenance of environmental quality is insisted upon can justice be done. If it is possible to pass the costs of production along to others, it will inevitably happen. And if it is possible to enjoy the benefits that nature has created for oneself alone, that too will occur. Finally, if people are allowed to be short-sighted, they will not look into the distance, and the future will be dim. Hence, property rights in land demand the fulfillment of obligations, both for their protection and for their justification.

NOTES

[1]There has been a recent rush of books on the topic of property rights in the decade since the works by Lawrence Becker, *Property Rights: Philosophic Foundations* (London: Routledge & Kegan Paul, 1977) and D.R. Denman, *The Place of Property: A New Recognition of the Function and Form of Property Rights In Land* (Berkhamsted: Geographical Publications Ltd., 1977). They are Alan Ryan, *Property and Political Theory* (Oxford: Blackwell, 1984); Andrew Reeve, *Property* (Atlantic Highlands: Humanities Press International, 1986); James 0. Grunebaum, *Private Ownership* (London: Routledge & Kegan Paul, 1987); Alan Ryan, *Property* (Milton Keynes: Open University Press, 1987); Jeremy Waldron, *The Right to Private Property* (Oxford: Clarendon Press, 1988); Alan Carter, *The Philosophical Foundations of Property Rights* (London: Harvester Wheatsheaf, 1989) and Stephen R. Munzer, *A Theory of Property* (Cambridge: Cambridge University Press, 1990).

Unfortunately, little or no attention is given to the relationship between property rights in land and environmental issues. Most concern themselves with the issue of justifying ownership. Grunebaum does make reference to the problem without ever discussing it at length. Denman focuses on the topic from the angle of redistribution and tenancy but with consideration of the environment. For my own, more extended treatment of the issues see Christopher Mooney, *Property Rights in Land: A Philosophical Analysis of the Rights and Responsibilities of the Ownership of Land* (Fordham University, unpublished PhD thesis, 1981).

[2]It has been pointed out that the famous speech by Chief Seattle that is often quoted for good effect is not authentic. At least not in the version with which most people are acquainted. See, Rudolf Kaiser, "Chief Seattle's Speech(es): American Origins and European Reception-Almost a Detective Story," paper presented to European Association for American Studies Biennial Conference, Rome, Italy, 1984. See, also, Rudolf Kaiser, "A Fifth Gospel, Almost: Chief Seattle's Speech(es): American Origins and European Reception," in Christian Feest, ed., *Indians and Europe: An Inter-Disciplinary Collection of Essays* (Aachen, Federal Republic of Germany: Rader Verlag, 1987). For good overviews, see, J. Baird Callicott, "Traditional American Indian and Western European Attitudes Toward Nature: An Overview", pp. 177-201 and "American Indian Land

Wisdom: Sorting Out the Issues", pp. 203-219 in *In Defense of the Land Ethic* (Albany: State University of New York Press, 1989). Also, Stewart Udall, "First Americans, First Ecologists," in Charles Jones, ed., *Look to the Mountain Top* (San Jose, Cal.: The H.M. Gousho Co., 1972) pp. 2-12; J. Donald Hughes, "Forest Indians: The Holy Occupation," *Environmental Review 2* (1977): 2-13; Terrence Geieder, "Ecology Before Columbus," *Americas 22* (1970): 21-28; G. Reichel Dolmatoff, "Cosmology as Ecological Analysis: A View From the Rainforest," *Man 2* (1976): 307-318; William A. Richie, "The Indian and His Environment," *New York State Conservationist Journal 10* (1955-56): 23-27; Thomas W. Overholt, "American Indians as Natural Ecologists," *American Indian Journal 5* (September 1979): 9-16.

[3]The material on Thoreau is too large to cite. For Aldo Leopold, see *A Sand County Almanac* and *Sketches Here and There*, (New York: Oxford University Press 1987) and Arran, *Companion to a Sand County Almanac*, ed. J. Baird Callicott, (Madison: University of Wisconsin Press, 1987).

[4]C.J. Glacken, *Traces on the Rhodian Shore* (Berkeley: University of California Press, 1967) is perhaps the most interesting study of man's ambivalent attitude towards his environment.

More recent works include Robin Attfield, *The Ethics of Environmental Concern* (New York: Columbia University Press, 1983); Andrew Brennan, *Thinking About Nature* (Athens: University of Georgia Press, 1988); Robert Elliot and Gare, editors, *Environmental Philosophy* (University Park: Pennsylvania State University Press, 1983); Tom Regan, ed., *Earthbound* (Philadelphia: Temple University Press, 1988); Mark Sagoff, *The Economy of the Earth* (Cambridge: Cambridge University Press, 1988); and Paul W. Taylor, *Respect for Nature* (Princeton: Princeton University Press, 1986).

[5]Aside from the growing group of environmentalists, the most significant legal scholar has been Christopher Stone whose seminal work *Should Trees Have Standing? Toward Legal Rights for Natural Objects* (Los Altos, Calif: Kaufmann, 1974) is a classic. See, also, his *Earth and Other Ethics* (New York: Harper & Row, 1987).

In addition, see, Donald W. Large "This Land is Whose Land? Changing Concepts of Land as Property," *Wisconsin Law Review*, (1973):

1027-1082; Lawrence Tribe, "Ways Not to Think About Plastic Trees," *Yale Law Journal* 83 (1974): 1315-48; Victor John Yannacone, Jr. "Property and Stewardship—Private Property Plus Public Interest Equals Social Property," *South Dakota Law Review* 23 (1978): 71-147.

[6]S.R. Eyre, *The Real Wealth of Nations* (New York: St. Martin's Press, 1978).

[7]That there is a long tradition of land use controls in American history cannot be denied. See Harry N. Scheiber, "Property Law, Expropriation, and Resource Allocation by Government," 1789-1910, *Journal of Economic History*, 33 (1973): 232-251. For further discussion and reference, see, Paul W. Gates, "An Overview of American Land Policy," *Agricultural History*, 50 (1976): 213-229.

[8]*The Declaration of Governors for Conservation of Natural Resources*, pp. 186-88 in I. Burton and R.W. Kates, eds., *Readings in Resource Management and Conservation* (Chicago: University of Chicago Press, 1965).

[9]The literature on the topic is extensive, if inconclusive. See, A.I. Melden, ed., *Human Rights* (Belmont, Calif.: Wadsworth, 1970); Richard Flathman, *The Practice of Rights* (Cambridge University Press, 1975); D.D. Raphael, *Political Theory and The Rights of Man* (Bloomington: Indiana University Press, 1967); Eugene Kamenka and Alice Erh-Soon Tay, eds., *Human Rights* (New York: St. Martin's Press, 1978); Alan S. Rosenbaum, ed., *The Philosophy of Human Rights: International Perspectives* (Westport, Conn.: Greenwood Press, 1980). Tibor R. Machan, *Human Rights and Human Liberties* (Chicago: Nelson Hall, 1975); Murray N. Rothbard, *The Ethics of Liberty* (Atlantic Highlands, N.J.: Humanities Press, 1982); Theodore M. Benditt, *Rights* (Totowa, N.J.: Rowman and Littlefield, 1982); Loren E. Lomasky, *Persons, Rights and the Moral Community* (New York: Oxford University Press, 1987) and L.W. Sumner, *The Moral Foundation of Rights* (Oxford: Clarendon Press, 1987). For my own views, see Christopher P. Mooney, "The Nature of Rights," *Nassau Review*, 4 (1984): 56-67.

[10]Simone Weil, *The Need for Roots* (New York: Harper & Row, 1971), 3. W.D. Ross, *The Right and the Good* (Oxford: Clarendon Press, 1930) discusses the sense in which rights and duties are correlative on pages

48-56, and he makes the point that it would be "wrong to describe either legal or moral rights as depending for their existence on their recognition, for to recognize a thing (in the sense in which 'recognize' is here used) is to recognize it as existing already. The promulgation of a law is not the recognition of a legal right, but the creation of it, though it may imply the recognition of an already existing moral right. And to make the existence of a moral right depend on its being recognized is equally mistaken. It would imply that slaves, for instance, acquired the moral right to be free only at the moment when a majority of mankind...formed the opinion that they ought to be free...", 50-51.

[11]See J. Baird Callicott, "Elements of an Environmental Ethic: Moral Considerability and the Biotic Community" pp. 63-73, "The Conceptual Foundations of the Land Ethic" pp. 75-99, and "The Metaphysical Implications of Ecology" pp. 101-114, in *In Defense of the Land Ethic*, op.cit.

[12]However, Mark Sagoff is correct to point out that *hysteresis* causes people to feel greater loss when they are deprived of a good which they have enjoyed than what they feel when restricted or denied access to something they never grew accustomed to. "Men generally fix their attentions more on what they are possessd of, than on what they never enjoyed: For this reason, it would be greater cruelty to dispossess a man of any thing than not to give it him." David Hume, *A Treatise of Human Nature*, Book 3, pt. 2, sec. 1 (in L.A. Selby-Bigge, ed. [New York: Oxford University Press, 1978], p. 482). For a discussion of hysteresis, see R. Hardin, *Collective Action* (Chicago: University of Chicago Press, 1982), p. 82.

[13]See, Richard A. Epstein, *Takings* (Cambridge: Harvard University Press, 1985) for a vigorous defense of exclusive private property rights. His concluding chapter (pp. 331-35), "Philosophical Implications," fails to deliver its promise, however, and merely begs the question by insisting that two wrongs don't make a right. The assumption throughout the text is that property rights are, and must remain, as exclusive and absolute as possible.

[14]Bernard H. Siegan, *Economic Liberties and the Constitution* (Chicago: University of Chicago Press, 1980) attempts to counter Bruce Ackerman, *Private Property and the Constitution* (New Haven: Yale

University Press, 1977) which makes a strong case for greater regulation of property on constitutional grounds and legal precedent.

[15]Paul W. Gates, "An Overview of American Land Policy," *Agricultural History*, 50 (1976): 229.

[16]See, Herman E. Daly, ed., *Economics, Ecology, Ethics: Essays Toward a Steady-State Economy* (San Francisco: W.H. Freeman and Co., 1980); Warren A.Johnson and John Hardesty, eds., *Economic Growth vs. the Environment* (Belmont, Calif.: Wadsworth Publishing Co., 1971); Richard G. Wilkinson, *Poverty and Progress: An Ecological Perspective on Economic Development* (New York: Praeger, 1973); William Ophuls, *Ecology and the Politics of Scarcity: Prologue to a Political Theory of the Steady State* (San Francisco: W.H. Freeman and Co., 1977).

[17]E.F. Schumacher is perhaps the best known spokesman for this view. See, his *Small Is Beautiful* (New York: Harper & Row, 1973) and *Good Work* (New York: Harper & Row, 1979).

[18]John Ruskin, "Munera Pulveris," in *Words of Ruskin*, edited by E.T. Cook and Alexander Weddermen (London: G. Allen, 1903-12), 17:144.

[19]"Ethics and Economics in Environmental Law" in *Earthbound*, ed. Tom Regan, op.cit., p. 173.

[20]See R.I. Sikora and Brian Barry, eds., *Obligations to Future Generations*, (Philadelphia: Temple University Press, 1978) and Ernest Partridge, ed., *Responsibilities to Future Generations: Environmental Ethics* (Buffalo: Prometheus Books, 1981)

[21]John Passmore, *Man's Responsibility for Nature* (New York:Scribner's, 1974) distinguishes between these two problems: "Pollution," pp. 43-72 and "Conservation," pp. 7-100. He also discusses "Preservation," pp. 101-126. His tendency is to give more credit to technology and worry less about future possibilities than we would here, but the book is informative and philosophic.

[22]Letter dated September 6, 1789, pp. 488-493 in *The Life and Writings of Thomas Jefferson*, edited by Adrienne Koch and William

Peden, (New York: The Modern Library, 1944). On the question of whether the dead have rights or the interests against the living, see, Ernest Partridge "Posthumous Interests and Posthumous Respect," *Ethics*, 91 (1981): 243-264.

[23]R.H. Coase, "The Problem of Social Cost," *Journal of Law and Economics* 3 (October 1960). H.P. Green, "Cost-Benefit Assessment and the Law," *George Washington Law Review* 45 (5) (August 1977): 904-5; see also E.J. Mishan, *Cost-Benefit Analysis* (New York: Praeger, 1976), pp. 160-61.

[24]E.J. Mishan, *Technology and Growth: The Price We Pay* (New York: Praeger, 1969), p. 36.

[25]Garrett Hardin, "The Tragedy of the Commons," *Science*, 162 (1968): 1243-1248. Hardin has written extensively on this topic and allied subjects. Not surprisingly, some of his statements have proven to be very controversial. See his *Stalking the Wild Taboo*, 2nd ed. (Los Altos: William Kaufmann, 1978) and *Naked Emperors* (Los Altos: William Kaufmann, 1982).

ETHICAL THEORY AND SOCIAL STRATEGY
In Response to Mooney

By David A. Sprintzen
Long Island University
C.W. Post Campus

Professor Christopher Mooney places the discussion of "Property Rights and the Environment" on the proper footing when he notes that "property rights... are just as open to regulation and limitation as any other form of rights..." It is essential that property rights not be treated as absolute and inviolable, if there is to be any serious effort to develop a moral framework that can constructively assist us in establishing a viable long-term relationship between human life and the natural conditions that make it possible.

There is an unfortunate tendency in social and political theory — certainly in its most "popular" formulations in the United States — to begin with a warped "Lockean" notion of the individual and his/her rights, and to proceed to argue that society does not have the right to interfere with property that accrues to an individual as a result of having "mixed" his/her labor with it. Without here entering into a detailed analysis of the application of Lockean theory — including its constraining condition concerning there being "as much and as good" left for other's use — Mooney is certainly right to insist that "the right to 'destroy' one's property may apply to chattel, but it cannot apply to land." And he well — though a bit too vaguely — concludes that "there are greater responsibilities of law than seeing that every owner of land can reap as much profit from his site without worrying about the long-term consequences to society as a whole."

The central point to underline is that rights are the result of social agreement as to those concerns that are to be guaranteed respect and defended with the force of law — itself a social institution. There may be reasons that point toward (at least partially) socially transcendent realities, including ecology and human nature, but it is only within and through social organization that rights find expression and become enforceable. From this it follows that rights must be socially justified and placed in relation to one another. When this fact is joined with the now indisputable evidence concerning the social generation of the self, self-consciousness, and personal identity, the psuedo-Lockean doctrine of absolute property rights will clearly be seen, and should be treated, as nothing more than what in fact it is, a partially veiled ideological effort to justify vastly unequal shares of wealth. Once its pseudo-respectability is revealed, we can begin to address the intellectually serious and worthwhile questions concerning the scope and proper role of property rights in relation to other personal and social rights, duties, and goods. In this context, that means focusing our attention on the requirements for ecologically sustainable economic development and ethically defensible social institutions and values.

Once again Mooney is right when he observes that "...Western societies ...elaborate systems of property rights in land... are at the root of much of the difficulty" involved in our efforts to develop an adequate system of "environmental responsibility." But he does not seem to be entirely clear whether he is seeking an adequate theory or an effective social strategy — or is it a theory as a pre-condition of, or contribution to, such strategy? This problem emerges in his opening paragraph where he seems to shift uncritically from a concern with "develop(ing) an environmental ethic" to seeking "practical measures (that) will best resolve these issues." The relation between ethical theory and practical strategy is a highly complex and very important issue that Mooney's paper at best skirts — when it does not actually confuse. That confusion finds expression in several key places, as he completely fails to address the ideological relation between ethical and social theory, on the one hand, and class and institutional location, on the other. Note his off-hand observation that many are being "encouraged" to "imitate the American lifestyle," without any consideration as to "who" is doing that encouraging and how they may stand to benefit from it. Or his observation that "so long as the courts ground their decisions upon reasonable premises, they need not worry about public reaction." Or his belief that "objectively considered... it is hard to see how anyone can rationally oppose greater vigilance in enforcing environment controls." Unless he means to define, for example, "rationally" in some clearly self-serving or ideological manner, any careful observer must acknowledge that there is and will continue to be very serious theoretical and practical struggles over what constitutes appropriate "environmental controls," "vigilance," and "reasonable premises." In short, the issues of power and ideology are not well addressed in this paper.

Nor, for that matter, is the analysis of social causation. But two examples. Mooney explains the inadequacy of present environmental regulations as due to "the difficulty of overcoming the inertia created by the tremendous speed in which the huge industrial world has been moving against the fragile ecosystem of this lovely planet." But vague or poetic words do not replace the need for precision, argument, and evidence. Is it "the hugh industrial world" that is cutting down the Brazilian rainforests, for example, or pressing for nuclear power and mass-burn incinerators, or is it not rather fairly specifiable industrial, financial, and political interests?

Mooney also claims that "the lack of carefully monitored land use regulations... can be at least partially blamed upon an ill-conceived conception of property rights in land." That may be true — at least "partially" — but it is not at all clear from the analysis how that might work, how revised conceptions might make a difference, or what constitutes a "reasonable" notion that will "reflect both economic and ethical requirements." Once again, the ideological and political issues are totally overlooked, subsumed under the vague rubric of the "reasonable," without any analysis of how to obtain it, nor how it might make a difference once obtained.

Mooney's central arguments focus on four key issues: entrenched attitudes toward property rights; competing conceptions of economic efficiency; conflicts over responsibilities to future generations; and evaluation of "social costs." We have discussed some of the weaknesses of his discussion of entrenched attitudes. He well criticizes standard economic conceptions of "efficiency" — and appropriately quotes E.J. Mishan to the effect that "what constitutes a cost to commercial enterprise depends upon existing law." But he falls victim to precisely such "entrenched attitudes," seriously weakening the theoretical base of his paper, when he uncritically assumes that "maximum utilization" of land and its resources is the ideal goal of any system of property rights. The quantification implicit in that formulation should have raised some questions for him in the light of his latter assertion that "not all values can be given quantitative rankings." I am also reminded of the language of a recent Master Plan for the Town of Oyster Bay on Long Island that referred to a "parcel" as "underutilized and in need of development." A judgement, needless to say, that I and many others did not share. "Underutilized" by whom? it should be asked. And who feels that "need" to develop it? Thus, issues of quality as well as those of power and interest need to be addressed in a far more direct and developed manner.

But let me conclude on a more positive note. Says Mooney, "The most important point that needs repeating is... that the world is a place of finite resources, of diminishing returns. Even with the most efficient utilization of the earth and its fruits, we live in a time when conservation is an economic, as well as an ethical, imperative. And the time is fast running out." Of course, the Japanese and the Russians may still decide that it is more profitable to kill off the whales rather than to preserve them, but internationally organized opposition may bring sufficient pressure to bear to get them to yield. Or the United States may be "persuaded" to give up the rights to "mine" the seas and the Antarctic. But these will only stand a chance of happening if there is the widespread institutionalization of the kind of ecological consciousness for which Mooney argues. Whatever its weaknesses, his paper clearly takes its stand on the side of recognition of the finitude of natural resources, of the need to husband them for the long term — both for ourselves and our posterity — of the legitimacy of limiting claims to property in land in light of the social origins of the human being and of its rights and values, and ultimately of the ethical imperative of finding a moral theory consonant with the conjoint needs of human living and ecological habitability. For these contributions he is to be thanked.

ORGANISM, COMMUNITY AND THE "SUBSTITUTION PROBLEM"[1]

By Eric Katz
New Jersey Institute of Technology

I. INTRODUCTION

In this essay I examine two basic holistic models of natural systems —
organism and community — in order to determine their significance in the
formation of an environmental ethic. To develop a convincing, working
environmental ethic it will be necessary to have a model of the natural
environment that is both ecologically and ethically sound. Any such model
used by philosophers and decision-makers must be compatible with current
scientific theories concerning ecological systems.[2] In addition, this model
must be in accord with basic ethical presumptions regarding environmental
policy. An environmental ethic must not violate basic environmentalist
attitudes.[3]

I suggest here that an environmental ethic based on a holistic model
of nature as an organism is unconvincing or unworkable in the light of basic
principles or attitudes of environmentalists; that an environmental ethic
based on a model of a natural community is in accord with basic
environmentalist attitudes; and thus, that a community model will be more
acceptable to environmentalists and ethical decision-makers.

II. HOLISTIC DOUBLE VISION

It has been often noted that a truly environmental or ecological ethic cannot be exclusively based on either (a) the interests of the human population or (b) the interests of individual natural entities.[4] Instead, advocates of an environmental ethic must adopt a holistic or "total-field" view of natural systems, in which individual natural entities and humans are "conceived as nodes in a biotic web of intrinsically related parts."[5] In an environmental ethic the ecological system or the natural environment becomes morally considerable. Don E. Marietta, Jr., writes: "The basic concept behind an ecological ethic is that morally acceptable treatment of the environment is that which does not upset the integrity of the ecosystem as it is seen in a diversity of life forms existing in a dynamic and complex but stable interdependency."[6] The interdependency is what counts. The system as a whole — and not merely the individuals in the system — is of primary moral significance. A theory of environmental ethics, thus, takes seriously Aldo Leopold's maxim of moral action:" A thing is right when it tends to preserve the integrity, stability, and beauty of the biotic community. It is wrong when it tends otherwise."[7]

However, noting the systemic character of a holistic environmental ethic is not sufficient to develop a working set of moral guidelines. There are different kinds of systems, different models or metaphors that will be used to establish the specific rules of an environmental ethic. Leopold himself used two different models or metaphors — nature as a "community" and nature as an "organism."

Readers of Leopold are generally drawn to his emphasis on the environment as a "biotic community," as in the quotation cited above. His essay, "The Land Ethic," begins with a straightforward statement about the importance of the idea of community in any ethical system: "All ethics so far evolved rest upon a single premise: that the individual is a member of a community with interdependent parts." This premise is also the basis of an environmental ethic because "the land ethic simply enlarges the boundaries of the community to include soils, waters, plants, and animals, or collectively: the land."[8] The source of moral obligations, duties, and rules is the "community," extended now to include the entities in the natural world.

Leopold, however, also conceives of the land as an organism, modelled after a living individual. For Leopold, an environmental ethic "presupposes the existence of some mental image of the land as a biotic mechanism."[9] If the natural system is conceived as one biotic entity, it becomes easier to care for its continued life or health, to respect its interests, and to consider it as morally worthwhile. Thus, Leopold describes the "land" as a biotic pyramid, a highly complex organizational structure of various kinds of living and nonliving natural entities. The environment is "a sustained circuit, like a slowly augmented evolving fund of life."[10] It is a "collective organism."[11]

It is not the purpose of this essay to trace the development of Leopold's thought concerning the establishment of an environmental ethic. But the fact that Leopold had two different models or metaphors in describing the land ethic shows that even in the work of one influential author there can be various kinds of holistic accounts of the natural environment. This kind of equivocation can cause problems, however, once the implications of the models are brought to bear on ethics. The models of organism and community as applied to natural systems are quite different, and yield different and incompatible moral conclusions.

III. INDIVIDUAL AUTONOMY IN HOLISTIC SYSTEMS

The crucial difference between the concepts of community and organism as applied to ecological systems lies in the autonomy of the individual parts within the holistic system. The model of community implies that there is some autonomy for the individual members of the community, while the model of organism implies that the parts are not independent things. Even the terminology is revealing, for each individual in a community can be called a member because it exists both in its own right and as a functioning unit of a community. But the parts within an organism lack the autonomous existence and value of an individual in a community — they are parts, nothing more; they are not members, not individuals, but units or elements in an organic whole.

A comparison of a typical organic whole, a human body, and a typical community, a university, clearly demonstrates the distinction. The muscles, liver, the blood, and other parts of the human body are not independent beings with lives or value apart from their organic function. Their existence is due to the continuous functioning of the organic whole

57

of which they are a part. Although various organs of a human body can be removed and transferred to another human body, the organic part is not an independent being in its own right. Organs are not organisms. If an organ is not transferred fairly quickly into another human body — i.e., a similar organic whole — its existence will come to an end.

In a community such as a university, however, the individual members — students, faculty, buildings, laboratory equipment, library materials — have an existence and value both in themselves and as functioning parts in the community. For this collection of entities to function as a university, of course, all the parts must play their roles: students must attend classes, faculty members must teach and do research, the library must update and organize its collections. But all these parts of the university have an autonomous existence that can be separated from their functions in the university system. Members are not organs. Students and faculty have interests that transcend their roles as members of the university. In part, they have lives that are based on other communities: a student may have an outside job; a faculty member may also be a scoutmaster. But they also have interests that are valuable outside of a communal context. A student jogs; a professor gambles at the racetrack. Even the nonliving elements of the university need not be parts of the university to be meaningfully employed. The buildings might be used after school hours by groups not affiliated with the university; the library books bring knowledge to individuals outside the school. In sum, the various entities that make up the university community are not merely parts of a holistic system; each has an independent existence. In an organic system, however, the elements are merely parts of the organic whole; each lacks a meaningful independent existence.

The natural ecosystem is more similar to a community like the university than to an organic system like a human body. It is difficult to conceive of humans, plants, and inanimate natural objects as mere parts of one large organism. These autonomous entities participate in an ecological system but in addition have independent lives and functions. The entities in an ecological system have roles to play in order to maintain the natural order but they also perform functions on their own. Evolutionary theory teaches that all species strive for their own survival, but in doing so they contribute to the functioning of the natural system. Bees are attracted to flowering plants for nectar, food for the bees, but as a result they pollinate and maintain the survival of the plant species. Natural individuals, then, live and act for and in themselves and as members of a communal system. They pursue their own interests and also serve roles in the community. It is not at all clear that organs in an organism do this.

In addition, consider how individuals can be moved from one particular ecosystem and placed in a different ecosystem. They can be introduced into systems where they do not occur naturally — as "exotics" — and still thrive. They can even be removed from a "natural" ecosystem completely and placed in a zoo. But, as I mentioned above, the parts of an organism cannot transcend their natural organic role. Organs can be transplanted, but unlike the introduction of exotic species, the organ must be transplanted into a nearly identical organism; they cannot "live" on their own. The ability of natural individual organisms in an ecosystem to be moved (or to move on their own) into new environments shows that they are not simply parts of an organism — they are independent individuals which operate in a flexible system of communal harmony.

An organic model of natural ecosystems is therefore misconceived. J. Baird Callicott, for example, claims that one can differentiate three "orders" or "organic wholes:" single cell organisms, second-order multicell organisms (with "limbs, various organs, myriad cells"), and "biocoenoses," third-order organic wholes such as the natural environment that are "a unified system of internally-related parts."[12] But nothing is gained by this terminology, for it blurs the clear distinction between individual organic bodies and ecological systems composed of individual organic bodies.

I assume that Calliott and other environmentalist philosophers[13] conceive or speak of the natural environment or a particular ecosystem as an organic whole in order to emphasize ecological interdependency. As a corrective measure for the common anthropocentric belief that humans exist beyond the realm of natural processes, this organic model may be acceptable. But eventually the organism model overemphasizes the dependency of the individuals in the system. I am not here denying that there is a dependency. However, the value of natural entities should not be based solely on their dependent functioning in the holistic system.[14]

IV. INTRINSIC AND INSTRUMENTAL VALUE

Up to this point I have not proven that the community model of the natural environment is better or more plausible than the organism model.

59

I have merely relied on the intuitive appeal of relevant comparisons. I will argue next that the organic model leads to moral conclusions that are incompatible with basic environmentalist positions. The community model is thus superior, since it does not lead to problematic moral conclusions.

To show this, I must introduce the concepts of intrinsic and instrumental value, and examine the relationship between these two kinds of value and the concepts of organism and community. An entity has intrinsic value if the entity has value in itself, without regard to other entities, without regard to its effects on other entities. The intrinsic value of an entity is based on its own independent properties. To have intrinsic value it need not have any relationship with another entity; its value, after all, is intrinsic to it.[15] An entity has instrumental value if the value of the entity is a result of some function or use to which it is put. The function may depend on the independent, intrinsic properties of the entity, but the value of the entity is derived from its functional purpose and not its intrinsic properties. It is an instrument to be utilized in some fashion, and nothing more: the effect it has on other entities is the criterion of its value.

In an important sense, then, instrumental value is directly contrary to intrinsic value. An entity valued intrinsically requires no relationships with any other entities. An entity valued instrumentally is dependent on the existence of other entities and the functional relationships between these entities. Instrumental value is not intrinsic but extrinsic. It is a result of interdependent relationships that exist between entities. It is the value an entity has for other entities.

Conceived in this manner, these two kinds of value are related to the concepts of organism and community in significant ways. Instrumental value bears a marked similarity to the way in which the parts of an organism are related to the whole. Organic parts have no independent value — their value is derived from the entire functioning whole, the organism. The liver, muscles, and blood in a human body are important for what they do for the organic whole. They are not valuable in themselves, i.e., intrinsically, but only instrumentally in that they perform functions for other entities. Thus, the parts of the organism have value as parts of a system, just as an entity with instrumental value only possesses value through its functional relations with other entities. But in a community system the members have independent existence and value. They may have communal value (i.e., functional value for the community), but they also maintain

60

independent status and value in (conceptual) isolation from the rest of the community. Thus, because a member of a community can be considered as an autonomous individual, it is similar to an entity with intrinsic value; it possesses some value in itself without regard to other entities.

Of course, individual entities possess both kinds of value in different situations and contexts. A member of a community has intrinsic value in itself and instrumental value as a functioning part of a system. A university student, as an individual human being, possesses personal characteristics that give him intrinsic value. But as a student this individual serves a function that is valuable for the community of which he is a member: he attends classes, interacts with the faculty and uses the facilities of the campus. It is more difficult, however, to see how parts of an organism can have intrinsic value, for they derive their value only from the role they play as part of a larger organic system. A human liver, in general, has merely instrumental value as a functioning part of an organism.[16]

In sum, the model of community permits the consideration of both intrinsic and instrumental value to a greater extent than the model of organism. The latter is primarily concerned with the functions of interdependent parts, and so it emphasizes instrumental value. Since a community is composed of autonomous members interacting towards a common goal, it allows for both kinds of value.

V. INTRINSIC VALUE AND THE SUBSTITUTION PROBLEM

It is my contention that only a mode of the natural environment that utilizes both the concepts of intrinsic and instrumental value is adequate for the operation of an environmental ethic. Only the use of both kinds of value will prevent moral conclusions that violate the spirit of environmentalism. But the preceding analysis has revealed that the model of organism is unable to accommodate both kinds. Since the model of community alone can employ both, the model used by an environmental ethic must be the idea of a natural community.

Unfortunately, other important analyses of the holistic structure of an environmental ethic have failed to stress the significance of intrinsic value.[17] I will cite one example. Paul Shepard writes:

Ecological thinking ... requires a kind of vision across boundaries. The epidermis of the skin is ecologically like a pond surface or a forest soil, not a shell so much as a delicate interpenetration. It reveals the self enabled and extended ... as part of the landscape and the ecosystem, because the beauty and complexity of nature are continuous with ourselves ... [w]e must affirm that the world is a being, a part of our own body.[18]

Shepard's metaphor that the natural world is a part of my body, and similarly, that my body is part of the organic structure of the natural world, is clearly an organic conception. But concentrating on the organic unity of the entities in the natural environment results in an emphasis on the instrumental value of entities in the organic system instead of on the intrinsic value of the entities in themselves.[19]

The overemphasis on the organic model for natural systems — with the resulting overemphasis on instrumental value — leads to a particular interpretation of the primary rule of action in an environmental ethic: the good for the natural system as a whole is the primary consideration. Callicott interprets Leopold's maxim — "A thing is right when it tends to preserve the integrity, stability, and beauty of the biotic community" — to mean that "the effect upon ecological systems is the decisive factor in the determination of the ethical quality of action."[20] This concern for systemic good tends to downgrade or even to ignore the intrinsic value of individual entities. Thus Callicott criticizes the advocates of animal rights for using the intrinsic evil of pain. It is not a proper consideration in the treatment of animals in natural ecological systems. Even if pain were an intrinsic evil, it is irrelevant from the point of view of systemic good. "Pain and pleasure seem to have nothing at all to do with good and evil if our appraisal is taken from the vantage point of ecological biology."[21] Pain and pleasure are intrinsically related to an entity in itself; they contribute nothing directly to the overall functioning of the natural system. The existence of intrinsic values in individuals can be ignored in the evaluation of the overall good for the natural system. The instrumental functional value of entities contributing to systemic well-being is given ethical priority. What is evil for individuals might be, and often is, a systemic functional good, and thus acceptable.

62

This organic model of the natural environment and its overemphasis on instrumental value leads to unacceptable moral conclusions. It falls prey to a serious moral problem which I call "the substitution problem." If an entity in a system is valued for its instrumental function and not its intrinsic value, then it can be substituted for or replaced as long as the function it performs remains undisturbed. In other words, if an entity is considered valuable because of its functional role in the system, then what is really important is the role, and if an adequate substitute can be found, then the entity itself can be destroyed or replaced without loss of value. Nothing is lost for the overall good of the system. As long as the system is maintained, the precise character or intrinsic worth of the particular individual performing its functions is irrelevant.

Perhaps there are no "pure" cases of the substitution problem, an instance in which one species or entity is substituted for another with no other changes in the natural system. But this kind of substitution is a logical possibility, and it is useful as a thought experiment. Something like the substitution problem must occur in nature, for ecological competition concerns the conflict of species over a particular ecological niche in the system. Often one species drives out another with little or no change in the overall functioning of the natural environment. The ecological niche is filled by a different species which assumes the role of its defeated competitor; the natural system is maintained. Our human knowledge of ecology might reach the point where non-natural substitutions of natural species could be made with little or no damage to the natural system. These substitutions will be morally acceptable policies of action in any organic model. But these substitutions clearly violate the spirit of environmentalism. Destroying and replacing a natural entity is not what environmental protection is all about.

There are related examples of the problem that are not merely theoretical. Lilly-Marlene Russow and John Passmore, for example, each discuss the possibility of modifying an existing ecosystem by increasing its diversity. Russow criticizes any environmental ethic based on the overall good of the natural community. This kind of ethic seems to allow "changes which do not affect the system, or which result in the substitution of a richer, more complex system for one that is more primitive or less evolved."[22] The institution of "changes which do not affect the system" and the idea of creating more complex systems are both versions of the substitution problem. Russow cites the introduction of new species in isolated areas (such as New Zealand and Australia) that replace the

63

indigenous species and create a new, workable ecosystem.[23] An environmental ethic based on the good of the natural ecosystem cannot prohibit this modification of nature, for the new ecosystem is successful, and the life of the natural entities in the system continues. But surely there is something wrong with this kind of modification.

Passmore considers whether ecological diversity can be a moral criterion. He argues from a human-centered perspective that increasing or decreasing species diversity can be either good or bad — depending on the factual circumstances. Although the case that usually concerns environmentalists is the loss of diversity caused by the extinction of species, not all such extinctions are considered moral evils. The elimination of the smallpox virus was not condemned as a loss of ecological diversity.[24] Passmore considers the possibility of eradicating disease-bearing mosquitoes if this could be achieved without any ecological damage to the rest of the ecosystem.[25] In such a situation, the preservation of a mosquito species just for the sake of diversity appears to be a mistake. Similarly, with the addition of species: Passmore cites the introduction of the elm and oak in Britain, where the increased diversity led to a more beneficial and stable environment.[26] Depending on the circumstances, therefore, the increase or decrease in diversity can have good or bad consequences for the ecological system.

Granting that the overall system is not harmed, why do certain kinds of cases involving diversity strike an environmentalist as inappropriate? Why is the elimination of a thriving species or the artificial diversification of an ecosystem considered bad? The answer involves the ideas of identity, integrity, or intrinsic value of individual organisms and species. This set of ideas provides the key to understanding the "substitution problem." Artificial diversification of a natural system violates the "naturalness" of the system. It alters the system in a way that is not the outgrowth of natural evolutionary change. In a sense it imposes a human ideal on the operations of a nonhuman natural system. Passmore, for example, also thinks that a wilderness without flies would be better than a wilderness with flies. A hypothetical wilderness experience without bugbites would be more pleasurable and just as (spiritually) enriching as the wilderness experience as it actually is today.[27] But there is something terribly wrong with this kind of modification. The best way I can express this is to say that human modifications harm the intrinsic value of the entities contained within natural systems. Individuals within natural systems have intrinsic value

64

(among other reasons) by virtue of their existence in the natural world. Forcing these entities to conform to a human ideal, a human value, of what nature ought to be, would harm this intrinsic value. Thus, the modification of natural systems — even when the result is an increase in systemic well-being — is a violation of the intrinsic value of natural entities.

In other words, what I am suggesting is that part of what we mean by the intrinsic value of natural entities is their source or origin — what caused them to be what they are. A natural entity possesses intrinsic value to some extent because it is natural, an entity that arose through processes that are not artificially human. This "naturalness" is one of the properties that gives it its value. Robert Elliot makes this same point about natural entities by comparing them to works of art. A technically perfect reproduction of a work of art lacks the value that the original has because of its "causal genesis."[28] But art reproductions are a fine analogue to instances of the substitution problem. A technically perfect art reproduction functions as well as the original; what it lacks is the same intrinsic value because it is a copy, a fake, a forgery; it is not the product of the original artist's creative process. The same is true for natural entities: a technically adequate functional substitute, because it is not an outgrowth of the original natural process of the system, lacks the same intrinsic value as the original entity.

Moreover, the violation of individuals' intrinsic value ultimately affects the integrity or value of the system as a whole. When the individuals are changed, when substitutions are made, the system becomes different. Consider a case involving a human system. A school administrator wants to increase the overall reading level of his school. Rather than hire more remedial reading tutors, he simply transfers into his district several dozen students who are much better readers than average. To make room for these students, he suspends some of his worst students for a semester. Something is wrong with this "artificial substitution" of individuals. Although the reading scores go up, although the system is improved, there has been a violation of individual and systemic intrinsic value and integrity. The source of the change has violated the system's intrinsic value.

Finally, consider the preservation of rare and endangered species. Russow notes that the preservation of rare species — particularly those that have been removed almost entirely from their natural habitats — cannot be justified by an appeal to ecological well-being, to the functional value these individuals provide the ecosystem.[29] Such individuals are no longer really part of an ecological system. They have no instrumental value, since the ecological system seems to function quite well without them.[30] Thus, if they are to be preserved or protected, as environmentalist policies universally dictate, it must be because of their intrinsic value. What makes this conclusion interesting is that cases of rare and endangered species can be considered to be instances of the substitution problem, so to speak, in midstream. A species becoming extinct was once a functional member of the natural system; it had instrumental value for it occupied an ecological niche in the system. Its' present endangered state is a result of some kind of substitution — either it lost an evolutionary-biological battle with a more competitive species that is replacing it, or it has been displaced by artificial human modifications of the environment. The fact that the completion of the substitution process — the extinction — is viewed by environmentalists as a wrong to be prevented shows clearly that the intrinsic value of the species is a prime consideration of environmental decision-making.

At the core of the "substitution problem," then, lies the idea of intrinsic value in a natural system. To take a well-functioning ecological system and replace one entity or species with another, to increase or decrease the diversity of the ecological structure, to fail to prevent or even to aid the extinction of the species — all these actions compromise the intrinsic value of the entities in the system. An environmentally conscious moral decision-maker cannot merely consider the instrumental value, the functional operation of the entities in the ecological system; he must also consider the integrity and identity of the entities in the system, i.e., their intrinsic value.

VI. CONCLUSION

Consideration of the substitution problem suggests that the community model of the natural environment is superior to the organic model as the guiding metaphor of an environmental ethic. If an environmental ethic uses the model of organism, it will be unable to account for the intrinsic value of the individuals in the system, and so it falls prey to the substitution problem.

Let me conclude with the words of Leopold: "A land ethic changes the role of *Homo sapiens* from conqueror of the land-community to plain member and citizen of it. It implies respect for his fellow-members and also respect for the community as such."[31] We must take Leopold quite seriously on this point. An environmental ethic must take into account the good for the community as a whole, and the good for each and every member of the community as an individual. The community model of nature can do this, and thus it results in a modification of a purely holistic ideal. A practical and meaningful environmental ethic will thus require a definite formula for the balancing of instrumental and intrinsic value criteria relative to individuals in a system. This is a task that remains to be done; but it cannot be even considered from the organic holistic perspective.[32]

NOTES

[1]An earlier version of this paper was read at a conference, *"Environmental Ethics: New Directions"* sponsored by the journal *Environmental Ethics* and the University of Georgia, October 5th, 1984. A longer version of this paper appeared in *Environmental Ethics* 7 (1985): 241-256. The author wishes to thank Holmes Rolston and J. Baird Callicott for their assistance on an earlier version of this paper.

[2]I do not mean to raise the specter of the fact-value problem. This problem is pervasive throughout the literature on environmental ethics, and I cannot address it here. See E.M. Adams, "Ecology and Value Theory," *Southern Journal of Philosophy* 10 (1972): 3-6; Thomas B. Colwell, Jr., "The Balance of Nature: A Ground for Human Value," *Main Currents in Modern Thought* 26 (1969): 46-52; Holmes Rolston, "Is There an Ecological Ethic?" *Ethics* 85 (1975): 93-109; Rolston, "Are Values in Nature Subjective or Objective?" *Environmental Ethics* 4 (1982): 125-151; and J. Baird Callicott, "Hume's Is/Ought Ethic." *Environmental Ethics* 4 (1982): 163-174. What I am saying here is much simpler. A workable environmental ethics cannot violate scientific laws about the operation of ecological systems. An environmental ethic that prescribed pollution (scientifically described) would be absurd.

[3]I mean *basic* attitudes. Obviously, there are many different kinds of environmentalists, with different ideas about the use and preservation of the natural environment. I make no dogmatic assumptions about what constitutes an environmentalist. I do assume, however, that the careful use and protection of natural resources, the control of pollution, and the preservation of endangered species are the broad heart of the position. In this light, the differences between Garret Hardin, Barry Commoner, David Brower, and Edward Abbey — to name just a few — are matters of degree.

[4]This literature is too vast to be noted completely. For the general character of an environmental ethic, see Rolston and Colwell in Note 1. See also Don E. Marietta, Jr., "The Interrelationship of Ecological Science and Environmental Ethics," *Environmental Ethics* 1 (1979): 195-207, and J. Baird Callicott, "Animal Liberation: A Triangular Affair," *Environmental Ethics* 2 (1980): 311-338.

An environmental ethic cannot be based on human interests because of the contingent relationship between human interest and the welfare of the natural environment. For a discussion of this point see Martin H. Krieger, "What's Wrong with Plastic Trees?" *Science* 179 (1973): 446-455; Laurence H. Tribe, "Ways Not to Think About Plastic Trees," *Yale Law Journal* 83 (1974): 1315-1348; Mark Sagoff, "On Preserving the Natural Environment," *Yale Law Journal* 84 (1974): 205-267; Sagoff, "Do We Need a Land Use Ethic?" *Environmental Ethics* 3 (1981): 293-308;Christopher Stone, *Should Trees Have Standing? Toward Legal Rights for Natural Objects* (Los Altos, CA: William Kaufmann, 1974); William Godfrey-Smith, "The Value of Wilderness," *Environmental Ethics* 1 (1979); 308-319; and my "Utilitarianism and Preservation," *Environmental Ethics* 1 (1979): 357-364.

An environmental ethic cannot be based on the interests of individual natural beings because many natural entities worth preserving are not clearly the possessors of interest. These nonliving and nonsentient beings acquire moral standing through membership in a holistic system. See Kenneth E. Goodpaster, "On Being Morally Considerable," *The Journal of Philosophy* 75 (1978): 308-325; Goodpaster, "From Egoism to Environmentalism," in *Ethics and Problems of the 21st Century*, ed. K.E. Goodpaster and K.M. Sayre (Notre Dame: Univ. of Notre Dame Press, 1979), pp. 21-35; Bryan G. Norton, "Environmental Ethics and Nonhuman Rights," *Environmental Ethics* 4 (1982): 17-36; and my "Is There a Place for Animals in the Moral Consideration of Nature?" *Ethics and Animals* 4 (1983): 74-87.

[5]Godfrey-Smith, p. 316. He cites Arne Naess, "The Shallow and the Deep, Long-Range Ecology Movement. A Summary," *Inquiry* 16 (1973), 95-100.

[6]Marietta, p. 197.

[7]Aldo Leopold, "The Land Ethic," in *A Sand County Almanac* (1949; reprint New York: Ballantine, 1970), p. 262.

[8]Ibid., p. 239.

[9]Ibid., p. 251.

¹⁰Ibid., p. 253. The full discussion is on pp. 251-261.

¹¹Ibid., p. 261. Although the idea of the natural environment as an organism or biotic mechanism is only a subordinate theme in "The Land Ethic," it was obviously central to Leopold's thought. In an essay published after his death (but written some twenty-five years before "The Land Ethic"), Leopold wrote that "in our intuitive perceptions ... we realize the indivisibility of the earth — its soil, mountains, rivers, forests, climate, plants, and animals, and respect it collectively not only as a useful servant but as a living being, vastly less alive than ourselves in degree, but vastly greater than ourselves in time and space..." (Aldo Leopold, "Some Fundamentals of Conservation in the South-west," *Environmental Ethics* 1 (1979): 140). This organic conception of the natural environment as a vast living being was an integral aspect of Leopold's vision; it was indispensable to his development of a primitive environmental ethic. (See Callicott, "Animal Liberation," p. 322, note 26:".... a rereading of 'The Land Ethic' in the light of 'Some Fundamentals' reveals that Leopold did not entirely abandon the organic analogy in favor of the community analogy.")

¹²Ibid., p. 321, and note 25.

¹³See, for example, Paul Shepard, "Ecology and Man — A Viewpoint," in *The Subversive Science*, ed. Paul Shepard and Daniel McKinley (Boston: Houghton Mifflin, 1969). pp. 2-3. Shepard is discussed below in the text.

¹⁴In reviewing an earlier version of this paper, Callicott was severely critical of the preceding section of the argument. As a means of making the argument clearer, I will attempt a brief summary of Callicott's criticisms and an answer to them.

Callicott has two major complaints regarding my contrast of the models of organism and community, and the subsequent comparison of community and natural ecosystems. First, he claims, that I misrepresent the model of organism by focusing on the parts of an organism or organs rather than cells. If we consider a "cellular model" of organism, the parts of the organism gain a substantial amount of autonomy. Cells can be more easily transferred than organs. Now I agree that the cells in an organism are more autonomous than organs — but this only makes the "cellular-model" of organism more akin to a community model. Callicott's cellular view of organic parts is simply another form of community, and it gains its plausibility from its affinity with a communal model. Second, Callicott claims that my argument is only plausible because I have limited my discussion to "micro" holistic systems — a university instead of society *per se*, a natural ecosystem instead of the global biosphere. An organ cannot exist outside the global biosphere. These "macro" comparisons suggest to Callicott an organic approach. Yet even on this large scale, there are differences. An organic part must be transplanted into a nearly identical being — a human liver into a human body. But a social individual can be transferred into many different kinds of society. Although a twentieth century social being might perish if cut off from all society, he might still survive in an assortment of social frameworks: with Bedouins, monks in Tibet, the elite in Hollywood, or even a family of baboons. Members of a community — unlike organic parts — have a greater freedom to move and change their systemic places. This freedom is their autonomy, their difference from organic parts.

Finally, it is my intuition that the "larger" these models get the more implausible both of them seem to be. The entire biosphere is neither one organism or one community. To consider it such seems to result in a vague generalization — similar to the "brotherhood of man" — that does nothing to advance environmental ethics.

[15]I exclude from consideration the relationship between the entity and the perceiver of value (i.e., the consciousness aware of the intrinsic value). Although consciousness may be necessary for the existence of value (I leave this question open and do not address it here), it is still the case that consciousness can value an entity for what it is in itself, intrinsically.

Note also that I am not arguing that intrinsic value is a psychological state of an individual, as a Benthamite would. I do not know what intrinsic value is, and I do not specifically define it here. The precise characterization of intrinsic value awaits further study. All that I claim is that intrinsic value, whatever it is, is based on the entity's own properties. See for more discussion, Andrew Brennan, "The Moral Standing of Natural Objects," *Environmental Ethics* 6 (1984): 35-56, and the references in note 17 below.

[16]One might want to argue that a human liver is aesthetically beautiful, and that if beauty is an intrinsic value, that the liver thus possesses intrinsic value. But I think this kind of example is far-fetched. Although any existing thing could have intrinsic value based on its own individual properties, the predominant value associated with organic parts is instrumental value.

[17]Those that stress intrinsic value (for example, Tom Regan, "The Nature and Possibility of an Environmental Ethic," *Environmental Ethics* 3 (1981): 19-34; and Lilly-Marlene Russow, "Why Do Species Matter?" *Environmental Ethics* 3 (1981): 101-112) tend to abandon the holistic conceptions of an environmental ethic.

[18]Shepard, pp. 2-3.

[19]The work of Holmes Rolston is very important in this area. Rolston is sympathetic to both kinds of value, and yet he argues that when one considers natural systems the idea of intrinsic value tends to blur or fade into the idea of instrumental value: the idea that an entity can be evaluated "'for what it is in itself...' becomes problematic in a holistic web." The concept of intrinsic value ignores "relatedness and externality." Within a natural system, "things do not have their separate natures merely in and for themselves, but they face outward and co-fit into broader natures." (Rolston, "Are Values in Nature Subjective or Objective," pp. 146-47.) See also, Rolston, "Values Gone Wild,: *Inquiry* 26 (1983): 181-207.

[20]Callicott, "Animal Liberation," p. 320.

[21]Ibid., p. 332.

[22]Russow, p. 107.

[23]Ibid., p. 108.

[24]But see David Ehrenfeld, *The Arrogance of Humans* (New York: Oxford, 1978), pp. 207-211, where he does condemn this loss. The implication of my essay is that the loss of the smallpox virus would be a moral wrong, for it is a loss of intrinsic value.

[25]John Passmore, *Man's Responsibility for Nature* (New York: Scribner's, 1974), p. 119.

[26]Ibid., p. 120.

[27]Ibid., p. 107. Passmore writes: "But it is not at all clear that to sustain this (wilderness) experience the wild country needs to be a wilderness in the full sense of the word: were it, for example, to be purged of flies, I, for one, would not find the refreshment diminished. It is much easier to state a case for the preservation of the humanized wilderness as places of recreation than for the preservation of wilderness proper."

[28]Robert Elliot, "Faking Nature," *Inquiry* 25 (1982): 81-93.

[29]Russow, p. 107. For another discussion of the difficulty in justifying the preservation of rare species, see Alastair S. Gunn, "Why Should We Care About Rare Species?" *Environmental Ethics* 2 (1980): 17-37. Gunn demonstrates the impossibility of utilitarian (i.e., instrumental) argument for preservation of rare species, and suggests the importance of intrinsic value.

[30]Note that I am not discussing rare endangered species that are biologically important to an ecosystem. There are obvious reasons for preserving those kinds of endangered species. What interests me is why we should preserve species that are *not* biologically important.

[31]Leopold, "The Land Ethic," p. 240.

[32]I have attempted to balance the communal (instrumental) and the individual (intrinsic) moral criteria in an environmental ethic in "Is There a Place for Animals in the Moral Consideration of Nature?" See also Evelyn B. Pluhar, "Two Conceptions of an Environmental Ethic and Their Implications," *Ethics and Animals* 4 (1983): 110-127.

ENVIRONMENTALIST VALUES
In Response to Eric Katz

By Eric Walther
Long Island University
C.W. Post Campus

Dr. Katz has given us a most enlightening introduction to the philosophical issues that are interwoven with the foundations of environmental ethics. Under his guidance, our focus shifts with ease from comprehensive holistic metaphors which teach that the ecological system *as such* is morally considerable, to such exquisitely specific details as a wilderness without blackflies and the telos of a liver. His paper made a field with which I am little acquainted come alive with fascinating conundrums and fresh conceptual approaches. Here is one region of philosophy where the attempt to deepen and to clarify our initial valuations still holds the promise of surprising and powerful conceptual novelties.

I emphasize the freshness and novelty of this field, and Katz's success in conveying them, because my criticisms will focus on his use of a value typology which is of a strikingly opposite character: the hackneyed and shop-worn old distinction between instrumental and intrinsic values. I feel that the budding insights of this field cry out for less familiar concepts. That is why my comments will focus, perhaps ungenerously, on those points at which I think resort to the concepts of instrumental and intrinsic value has failed to clarify the moving insights in Katz's presentation.

The *intrinsic* value of an entity, says Katz, is based upon its own independent properties. In this connection, he thinks it is important to show that organisms can function independently of their usual ecological contexts. I don't understand why the properties upon which an entity's intrinsic value depends must be *independent* properties. Consider the bullfrog: his croaking behavior is arguably more independent of other components of the natural system than his egg-laying (in water) or his catching of flies; but all of these behaviors contribute in exactly the same way to essential bullfroghood. I should think that one who regards the bullfrog as having intrinsic value would regard *all* of its characteristic properties as contributory to that value, regardless of whether or not they are "independent" properties.

Katz says that to have intrinsic value, an entity need not have any relationship with another entity. I find that statement extremely puzzling. To abstract away from a bullfrog's relationships with other entities in the natural system is to *lose* most of what gives a bullfrog its intrinsic nature and value. A parasitic species is far less independent in its properties than a non-parasitic one; does it therefore have less intrinsic value? I don't see why an entity's ability to survive in alternative environments should have anything to do with its intrinsic value. In all of these respects, the conceptual ramifications of the term "intrinsic" seem to have imposed gratuitous burdens on Katz's account.

Actually, in emphasizing "intrinsic value," Katz may intend little more than that we value natural entities non-instrumentally. To value things instrumentally means to value them *only for their uses*; to value them intrinsically means to value them *for themselves* One who values bullfrogs solely as mosquito-eaters probably has the former attitude; one who loves their night-song is more likely to have the latter attitude. But the former attitude is totally foreign to environmentalist valuations. To emphasize that the value of natural entities is non-instrumental is hardly necessary, and it is misleading when it leads one to separate the vision of the bullfrog "as an independent entity" from the vision of the bullfrog "as a functional part of an ecosystem."

Katz seems to think that the functional parts of an ecosystem, considered as such, *can* have only instrumental value. Moreover, while his account of intrinsic values remains a bit vague, he has a very definite conception of what the instrumental value of natural entities consists in. A species within a natural system has instrumental value by virtue of the *use* to which it is put there; its effect on other entities is the criterion of its value. His most emphatic assertion is that a species has instrumental value because it occupies an ecological niche.

I think that this conception of instrumental value is deeply flawed, and invites inferences which Katz would surely oppose. Ecological niches are not holes which a system *needs* to have filled. Systems do not *use* their component members to achieve normative results. Attempts to apply these notions would immediately fall into absurdity. What would be the instrumental value of a rabbit — to crop excess greenery? To feed hawks? Does nature put the hawk to use in disposing of excess rabbits? Is it *bad* for the system to be overrun with rabbits? Everybody has heard that an excess of rabbits may be catastrophic, but it must provide wonderful opportunities for a few species. What norms of judgment are to be used in deciding what's bad for the system? Katz seems to think that the concept of intrinsic value suggests an answer. He says that the entities in an ecological system have roles to play *in order to* maintain the natural order. But this "order" is nothing but the stabilities and transitions inherent in the current ecological balance; there is no "in order to" here, no automatic presumption that it is somehow *good* or *fitting* or even *natural* that the extant stabilities should be maintained.

I am inclined to believe that there *are* valid environmentalist reasons for preferring some "natural orders" to others. When one construes the *existing* ecological functions of a natural entity in terms of instrumental value, however, one automatically invokes a normative attitude toward the existing system. I think that this error is a clear illustration of the inappropriateness of the traditional concept of instrumental value when interpreting the role of entities in an ecological system.

The analogy between organs in a body and functional parts of an ecosystem may contribute to this error. Katz argues that the analogy does not provide a complete or adequate basis for understanding natural communities; but he bases his account of instrumental values upon it. Before raising the question whether the analogy is adequate, we should consider whether it has any validity at all.

The instrumental value of the liver lies in its definable contribution to a state of the whole organism which is understood as *good for* the organism. Do rabbits and hawks contribute to a state which is similarly *good for* the ecosystem? Katz does make frequent reference to the "welfare" or "integrity" or "maintaining" of a natural system, but he does not analyze the concept. If hawks or rabbits or both disappear from an ecosystem in which they once thrived, the system will become *different*; but there is no clear and definite well-being for the system which is then compromised, in the way that health is compromised by a dysfunctional liver.

Actually, there is an interesting discrepancy in Katz's views on this matter. One would think that if an entity has instrumental value, then it is promoting some good which would be compromised by its absence. There is no natural health without natural disease. Katz admires ecological health, but he is unwilling to endorse any treatments of ecological disease unless the disease is anthropogenic! He states that the modification of natural systems is a violation of the intrinsic value of natural entities, even when the result is an *increase* in systemic well-being! We would be "forcing these entities to conform to a human ideal, a human value, of what nature ought to be." That is simply untrue if our actions are promotive of the *systemic* well-being which he has just referred to. If there *is* such a thing as systemic well-being, then our attempts to promote it need not be human-biased at all. But still, Katz continues, we would be damaging the "naturalness" of natural entities. This is probably so, in some sense which I still find very obscure. Katz, however, proceeds to link this "naturalness" with intrinsic value,and I can't see how the one has anything to do with the other. If we intervene in a way which increases or maintains species diversity, against natural tendencies toward species impoverishment, the more numerous species we thereby maintain are surely not lacking in those "independent properties of their own" to which Katz assigns intrinsic value.

I think that there are characteristic differences between the interventions which shock, and those which gratify, basic ecological sensitivities. I would like to see environmentalist theorists try to define those differences. To argue that *all* interventions violate "naturalness" is implausible. It may also be another case of being misled by expecting to derive usable environmentalist conclusions from the abstractions of intrinsic and instrumental values.

While reading Katz's concluding paragraph, I was struck by a contrast between the words used by Aldo Leopold and the words used by Katz in restating the point. Leopold speaks of the land ethic as teaching mankind "respect for his fellow-members (of the land-community) and also respect for the community as such." Katz restates this by saying that we need to take into account "the good for the community as a whole, and the good for each and every member of the community as an individual." What struck me was the very different impact of the words "respect" and "good." To *respect* the land-community: does that really amount to taking account of the *good* for the community? Is it the kind of respect which arises out of the recognition of goodness, or is it a respect which arises in some quite different way? I was reminded of what I regard as the high point in the *Euthyphro*. From an apparently hopeless beginning, Socrates has worked Euthyphro up to a level at which he can give quite a profound definition of piety: Piety has to do with the careful attention which is due to things divine; justice has to do with the careful attention which is due to things human. Unfortunately, Euthyphro is unable to remain at this level of insight, and his answers slip back into superstition and childishness. What Socrates was hinting at, I think, is the same notion that Hegel explored in his analysis of Antigone ("the ethical world" and "ethical action" in *The Phenomenology of Mind*): the divergence between the open, rational, man-centeredness of ethics,and the hidden, emotional, other-centeredness of religion.

To put it bluntly, I believe that the "respect" of which Leopold wrote, the "naturalness" whose nature Katz struggles to explain, and probably most of the fundamental insights of the environmentalist sensitivity, are at root matters of religious value, not matters of moral or ethical value. I am astonished when I find Katz remarking, in a footnote, that the loss of the smallpox virus is a *moral* wrong, because of the intrinsic value of that organism. (Intrinsic value, remember, is linked with the"naturalness" of an entity's existence within an ecosystem!). The assertion that eradication of the smallpox organism is a shock to appropriate *religious* attitudes of awe and respect toward nature seems more plausible. What is at issue seems more like a collision between different *types* of value, than like an opposition of claims which can be arbitrated within the category of moral right and wrong.

I intend this metaphysical suggestion to be taken in a pluralistic spirit. There is nothing dismissive in classifying environmentalist valuations as religious, if religious value and ethical/moral value are acknowledged as equally fundamental yet heterogeneous categories. That the instrumental vs.

intrinsic distinction is not helpful in an analysis of environmentalist valuations may be just one instance of a deep ambiguity concerning the fundamental nature of what we call, no doubt for want of a better term, environmental *ethics*. I want to end, however, by reiterating my initial remark: this field is made all the more exciting philosophically by the still-problematic character of its fundamental valuations. It will serve me right if Katz responds by demonstrating that my distinction between the religious and the moral is even more hackneyed, shop-worn and inappropriate than is his distinction between intrinsic and instrumental values!

RESPONDING TO SECOND GENERATION ENVIRONMENTAL CRISES

Keynote Address
by
Patrick G. Halpin
Suffolk County Executive

Ethics and the environment: an exceptionally topical topic. Hardly a day goes by when we are not confronted by yet another environmental catastrophe — often caused by unethical practices. From Bhopal to Love Canal; from the "bomb" to "star wars".

Forty years ago, Robert Oppenheimer, one of the fathers of the atomic bomb, viewed Hiroshima and Nagasaki and could only quote the Bhagavad Gita, saying "now I am become death, the destroyer of worlds." When it comes to the environment, "we have met the enemy and it is us."

Our technological abilities have advanced to the point where we can accomplish a world of things we once only dreamed possible. Men have walked on the moon. The United States is advancing the possibility of bringing the arms race into outer space. People are living while artificial hearts pump blood through their veins.

Our technological capabilities place us on the horns of an ethical dichotomy, for we are just as capable of working miracles as wreaking havoc and destruction. To government falls the task of making the decisions that advance life and sometimes cause death. We in government face an ethical choice: we can become the destroyer of our world, or we can work to save our world.

An ethical government must make a series of choices — especially concerning the environment. A healthy ecology is the foundation of a healthy life. Then how is it that environmental excellence is so often sacrificed in the name of progress?

The concept of "environment" is relatively new. It was first defined in the early 1970's as we developed an awareness of a world where water, air and land were carefully and delicately balanced, each in relation to the other. Until that time, we had viewed our world as being blessed with endless natural resources. As scientists investigated the effects of applications of pesticides, they discovered devastating side effects upon fish in rivers and lakes, and eagles nesting in trees. The "Silent Spring" made it apparent that the natural balance of entire ecosystems was being destroyed. We were horrified to learn that Lake Erie was "dead"; and to see pictures of the Cayahoga River, overflowing with chemicals and petroleum products, ablaze with flames.

As the widespread — indeed worldwide — effects of pollution became apparent, public concern and outrage grew. In the span of a decade the public's transition from "conservationist" to "environmentalist" was completed.

Beginning in 1970, a wide range of legislative initiatives to mitigate existing damage and prevent environmental devastation was begun. On the federal level, the Clean Air Act was passed, followed in rapid succession by the Clean Water Act; the Resource Conservation and Recovery Act; and the Safe Drinking Water Act. New York State followed suit, putting in place its own statutes and regulations aimed at environmental protection and preservation.

In 1970, the New York State Department of Environmental Conservation was created. Governor Rockefeller said "while state programs in the 1960's to clean up air, water and land pollution are ending a century

82

of neglect, this bill reflects the need now to consolidate and build upon these gains and set up effective machinery to avert future problems."

The '60's environmental concern opened the '70's floodgates of state environmental protection legislation. In 1972 the 1.1 billion dollar Environmental Quality Bond Act was passed, followed by the Tidal Wetlands Act and the State Pollution Discharge Elimination System in 1973. In 1975, the State Environmental Quality Review Act and the Freshwater Wetlands Program were established. In the late '70's, the Legislature began to address the problems stemming from toxic contamination with the passage of four major programs aimed at clean-up and disposal of hazardous wastes. In fact, in the past fifteen years, more than 1,000 New York State environmental laws have been passed; an average of 70 each year, or one each day that the Legislature was in session.

Against this backdrop, a political climate conducive to environmental accountability was nurtured and is now reaching maturity. As we struggled to define and understand the complexities of the "second generation" environmental crises we faced, we simultaneously grappled with how to resolve those problems. I say "second generation" environmental contamination crises because we have long since passed the obvious "first generation" of belching smokestacks and floating raw sewage. We are now confronted with more than 70,000 synthetic organic chemicals, oil derived chemicals, never before present in our environment. Only a handful of these chemicals have been tested to determine human toxic effects, cancer, genetic damage or birth defect potential. These "second generation" environmental threats are even more insidious since most often they cannot be tasted or seen. Yet, they open a Pandora's box of concern about public health risks. At the same time we have developed increasingly sensitive laboratory tests to detect contaminants in our environment. We can now detect chemical contaminants in the parts per billion and even parts per trillion. This is the equivalent of a single grain of salt in a football stadium of potato chips. And as we discover more and more chemicals in our environment we become less able to predict their effects on human health.

Let us consider, for example, the problem of PCB contamination of the Hudson River.

Small daily discharges of PCB's, a non-biodegradable chemical, from two General Electric facilities in the upper reaches of the Hudson have contaminated nearly 300 miles of the waterway. The PCB's accumulate in the flesh of fish and wildlife, making them inedible. A statewide health advisory is already in effect. Nursing mothers, pregnant women, infants and children under 15 are told not to eat any contaminated fish. These chemicals have also polluted the drinking water supplies of 150,000 people in the Hudson Valley.

PCB's in the Hudson demonstrate the interdependent nature of environmental protection and public health. Unless industry becomes environmentally responsible, the state's waterways will become irreversibly polluted. With the destruction of this irreplaceable natural resource follows not only the contamination of the drinking water of millions of New Yorkers, but also the demise of industries dependent on clean waterways: commercial fishing, tourism, sportfishing and other recreational opportunities.

The plight of the striped bass on the Eastern Seaboard provides an example of an industry thoughtlessly contributing to its own destruction.

Over the past twenty years, scientists have noted with increasing alarm the rapid decline of the striped bass: over 90% decline in the last ten years alone. Several causes have been attributed to this, including habitat degradation in the Chesapeake Bay, where spawned the vast majority of a once abundant striped bass population. But it also became increasingly apparent that the very popular food and game fish had been over-harvested; that the species was being caught before reaching maturity and reproducing; that the magnificent striper was in danger of vanishing forever.

Environmentalists, recreational fishermen, people from the federal government and representatives of all the states along the Eastern Seaboard from Maine to the Carolinas, joined together to produce a comprehensive management plan to prevent the extinction of the species. Following five years of effort, a solid management program was completed. Unfortunately, those who view their short-term business interests as threatened by an effort to conserve the striper worked to thwart its adoption and implementation. To this day, they continue to undermine our best efforts.

The short term goal of commercial fishermen is to catch as many striped bass as possible in order to make the highest profit possible. On today's market, a fisherman can sell these delicious tasting fish for three to four dollars a pound, making them among the most profitable to catch. But such shortsightedness produces long term ill effects. Results of a recent study have confirmed levels of PCB's in 90-99% of striped bass in excess of the allowable federal Food and Drug Administration limit of 2 parts per million.

Ironically, this treat to the public health may prove to be the deciding factor in the conservation of the species. A ban on striped bass fishing would allow more fish to reach maturity and propagate, and thereby replenish the stock. In effect, enforced ethics in the environment.

Another question involving ethics and our environment relates to garbage. New Yorkers witnessed and contributed to decades of discarding rubbish in so reckless a fashion that today the second highest point on Long Island is a landfill — a hugh Mount Trashmore of garbage. New Yorkers consistently threw away enough beer bottles and soda cans each year to fill Yankee Stadium four times over. With little thought to the economic or environmental consequences, we discarded ton after ton of reusable materials. Following a generation of this "throwaway society", people were fed up. As a member of the Suffolk County Legislature in 1981, I authored and succeeded in passing a Bottle Bill for Suffolk County. We became the first municipality in New York to require a deposit on beverage containers.

What a battle it was! Hoards of high paid attorneys and lobbyists from the headquarters of corporate giants such as Philip Morris, Anheuser Busch, 7Up and Pepsi Cola swarmed all over Suffolk County. In droves, they visited, pleaded and cajoled the legislators. "Our costs will rise", they begged, "consumers-costs will skyrocket", they threatened. "Jobs will be lost", they claimed. Last but not least, they said the Bottle Bill wouldn't work because the people didn't want it.

The debate was one of monied interests against environmental interests. As the industry got wind of this legislative initiative, the president of one of the area's largest firms paid me a visit. Ric Rose of Clair Rose, Inc. explained to me that the problem wasn't non-returnable bottles and cans, but that people are slobs. No matter what the incentive, he claimed, they would continue to litter. He was adamant on the point until he visited a couple of neighboring states that had in place a bottle bill — and he discovered that there was both a profit to be made and that people would return their empties. He discovered that an environmentally sound policy could be both effective and profitable.

In Suffolk County, we paved the way for passage of a statewide Bottle Bill. By the time I was elected to the State Assembly, 12 months after the adoption of the Suffolk County Bottle Bill, the political climate was right in Albany for passage of a statewide bill. It had taken almost ten years for that political stage to be set. Ultimately, Governor Hugh Carey — like many other New Yorkers — stepped on one too many pieces of broken glass while jogging in Central Park. He signed the Bottle Bill into law. The day of reckoning for those promoting pollution had come. The public demanded and government responded with public policy that protects the environment, and is also good business. A winning combination.

The success of the Bottle Bill is evident everywhere. Drive down any local street or highway, visit any park or beach, park in any municipal parking lot — once strewn with discarded cans and bits of broken glass. We have created hundreds of new jobs in New York State, boosted a sagging recycling industry, and created new markets for re-using what we once considered only garbage.

Just as a sound environment is essential for our health and well-being, so it is to sustain and encourage business. New York offers incomparable resources crucial for the success of industry: abundant water supplies and natural resources, an extensive infrastructure, access to markets, a skilled work force. Because of these opportunities, our state has a history of being among the most profitable places to do business anywhere in the world.

The public is environmentally aware, and our states' business community must follow suit. They have too often dragged their feet because it has been cheaper and easier to pollute; to think only of the short term.

For instance, a study undertaken by the Department of Environmental Conservation which will be released later this month, determined that more than 400,000 tons of hazardous waste is generated each year in New York State. The cost of properly disposing of this waste would be 57 million dollars a year. This is a small amount when compared to the billions it will cost to clean up the more than 1,000 illegal toxic waste dumps that have been discovered throughout the state.

With the passage of federal and state Superfund legislation, industry may soon begin to be forced to pay for the environmental damage they have wrought. Thoughtless and indiscriminate dumping of toxic waste once seemed economical to corporate chiefs concerned only with the next quarter's earnings. In actuality, pollution is lost product and lost profit and nothing less.

For business to reap hugh profits from pillage of the world that sustains us all is unacceptable. They must pay the price for past damage. It is not enough to clean up today's contaminants, industry cannot be allowed to contribute to tomorrow's pollution.

Long Island has become a battle ground for the environmental war we must fight across New York. Over the past eight years, Long Island has been rocked by a series of environmental contamination crises — some of which have set national precedents. The discovery, in 1976, of cancer causing chemicals in our groundwater; explosive levels of methane gas escaping from garbage dumps, and in one case killing a landfill worker; vinyl chloride gas, a known carcinogen, leaking from landfills and in one instance leading to the closing of a nearby elementary school; the discovery of PCB's in LILCO's natural gas lines; the closing of more than 1,000 East End wells due to Temik poisoning, the detection of dioxin in smokestack emissions at the Hempstead Resource Recovery Plant on Meadowbrook Parkway; hundreds of leaking, underground gasoline tanks, forcing scores of families from their homes; hundreds of homes contaminated by the termite pesticide chlordane.

Yet staffing levels at the State Department of Environmental Conservation remain woefully inadequate for the huge tasks confronting us. For instance, only one individual on Long Island oversees all 13 major municipal landfills to assure compliance with state and federal regulations. As a result D.E.C. performs in a haphazard fashion.

Since its inception, the Department's state funded purchasing power has decreased by over 27% after inflation. During this same 15 year period, the purchasing power of all state agencies increased nearly 18% faster than inflation. And, although federal disbursements have increased from 2

87

million dollars in 1971 to 34 million dollars in 1984, a number of the Department's programs are suffering from reductions in federal grants. For example, the Air Program lost over 1 million dollars from 1980 to 1984 resulting in a loss of 24 staff positions; non-hazardous waste grants were eliminated in 1982, and with them 50 staffers; and cuts to the federal Clean Water Act are expected to lead to still further staff reductions. In addition, New York State needs more than 3 billion dollars for sewage treatment, but only one third of that is available.

Technological capabilities have changed virtually everything about the world in which we live, except the way we think. Given the imperatives we face and the impending potential for unparalleled catastrophe, I suggest one major governmental change now. New York needs a state environmental agency that recognizes a new definition of "environment" and acts accordingly.

The tasks confronting the state agency charged with implementing policies aimed at statewide environmental protection and preservation have become increasingly complex, while the focus of the existing D.E.C. has become outmoded. Environmental protection can no longer be defined as conservation of fish and wildlife, parks and game preserved for future generations. The conservation movement begun almost a century ago has evolved into an ongoing struggle that must be waged simultaneously along many fronts.

I propose a first step toward solving an exceedingly complex problem. The D.E.C. should be split into two separate agencies — a Department of Conservation and a Department of Environmental Law Enforcement. The Department of Environmental Law Enforcement would be charged solely with developing, implementing and enforcing a statutory and regulatory framework for environmental protection. I suggest that we institutionalize what we have recognized to be a new set of "second generation" priorities.

New York is beginning to enhance its commitment to solving "second generation" pollution problems. By 1987, a one billion dollar bond act to clean up toxic waste sites and build resource recovery plants is slated to be put before the voters of the state for ratification; this year oversight of the Oil Spill Clean-up Fund was moved from the Department of Transportation to the D.E.C.; the 1985-86 State budget provides an increase in funding of

11.5 million dollars and 140 new staffers to the D.E.C. in an effort to enforce laws already on the books.

But we can not succeed in solving "second generation" problems with a "first generation" approach. The new Environmental Law Enforcement Agency that I propose would be an enforcement agency, and would provide technical coordination and information to assist in, for example, the development of resource recovery facilities. Today, the enforcement functions of the D.E.C. are provided by "environmental conservation officers." Not only is this a misnomer, it exemplifies a fundamental contradiction: a conservation officer has little time to knock at an industrial polluter's door when he is busy checking tags on deer. On the other hand, an environmental law enforcement officer would have the time, the authority and the resources to track down environmental criminals.

The proposed Department of Environmental Law Enforcement would engage in surveillance and investigation to stop illegal toxic waste dumping, prosecute polluters, and assure that permits programs are properly managed.

The Department of Environmental Law Enforcement would administer a bond act to help communities close landfills, build resource recovery plants, run recycling programs, complete sewage treatment plants, build hazardous waste treatment facilities and treat contaminated water.

In contrast, the proposed Department of Conservation would be just that. It would manage fish and wildlife resources, camping grounds, the forest preserves of the Adirondacks and Catskills, ski centers, wetlands, pine barrens, and be responsible for river and beach protection.

By separating the conservation and enforcement functions we would sharpen the focus of a too diffuse environmental protection effort and force a re-ordering of our governmental priorities — an ethical re-ordering of priorities.

The ethical re-ordering of New York's environmental protection priorities (as I see it and not being sacreligious) would entail following ten environmental commandments. They are:

1. Stop illegal toxic waste dumping.

2. Enforce environmental laws and permit programs.
3. Build resource recovery plants.
4. Close unlined solid and toxic waste dumps.
5. Build "state of the art" hazardous waste treatment facilities.
6. Complete sewage treatment programs.
7. Conserve water resources and treat contaminated water supplies.
8. Develop optimal recycling efforts.
9. Preserve pine barrens and our sole source aquifer.
10. Regularly test all drinking water supplies.

These ten environmental protection commandments are, as is the case with so many commandments, easy to enunciate but hard to live up to. Yet if we do not live up to them, we may not be able to live. The challenge facing us individually, and together as a society, is to change our way of living and thinking so that our environment supports us and we do not destroy it and ourselves in the process.

I thank you for your attention and look forward to working with you, and following the ten environmental protection commandments.

THE COMMERCIALIZATION OF NUCLEAR POWER: UNETHICAL BEHAVIOR ON A GRAND SCALE

By Theodore D. Goldfarb
S.U.N.Y. at Stony Brook

A group of entrepreneurs, who are interested in developing and selling a new product that may have adverse ecological or economic consequences, are faced with unavoidable choices with obvious ethical implications. Given the context of accepted values in our society, it would be naive to expect that such individuals would choose to be scrupulously careful about looking into all of the potential hazards inherent in the marketing of their product, nor to be excessively diligent about educating the public about even the more obvious anticipated problems.

When the product in question is a nuclear fueled electric power generating station, which during operation produces a quantity of lethal radioactive nuclei much greater than the radioactivity released by a megaton nuclear bomb and which requires a complex fuel cycle at every stage of which there is an additional possibility of environmental contamination by highly radioactive material, it is apparent that the public good requires absolute assurance of adequate protection. It is obvious that this is not achievable by relying on the ethical principles of those who seek to profit from this technology. Under such circumstances the citizens of a democracy

91

should expect that the needed protection would result from diligent regulation of all phases of the development of this uniquely hazardous energy source.

Unfortunately for all of us, the regulation of nuclear power by the United States Government was undermined from the beginning by serious conflicts of interest. Without public financing and promotion the business community would never have gambled the large sums of risk capital required to launch this problematic enterprise. There is documentary evidence that the decision announced to the country in President Eisenhower's Dec. 8, 1953 speech to strongly promote an "Atoms for Peace" program, with nuclear power as the centerpiece, was motivated by the political need to provide a cover for the further development of the increasingly unpopular nuclear warfare effort.[1] Lacking was any serious consideration of the problem that the government would have in providing the rigorous regulation of a new industry that it had now decided to sell, with the use of public funds, to a rather reluctant economic and industrial community.

The position of the Truman Administration following the devastation of Hiroshima and Nagasaki was that both military and civilian uses of atomic energy should be developed and controlled directly by the federal government. The Atomic Energy Commission (AEC) was created in 1946 and charged by Congress with overseeing this entire enterprise. During the late 40's and early 50's the AEC was preoccupied with managing the early days of the nuclear arms race. The efforts it made to promote nuclear power were ineffective as measured by the fact that by 1955 not one private utility had applied for a license for a nuclear power station.[2]

In 1954, responding to the urgings of the Eisenhower Administration, Congress revised the Atomic Energy Act to permit private companies to build and operate commercial nuclear power stations and plants to process waste materials.[3] The AEC was granted new authority to promote nuclear power and Lewis Strauss, a Wall Street investment banker and an enthusiastic advocate of privately developed atomic power was appointed to replace David Lillienthal as the agency's Chairman.[4] Strauss set about his new task with religious zeal initiating a "Power Reactor Demonstration Program" which he asserted was guided by "Divine Providence" as evidenced by the fact that a "Higher Intelligence decided man was ready to receive" the knowledge of the "atom's magnitude."[5] Ignoring the cautions

92

of numerous scientific and technical consultants to the AEC, Strauss urged the media to "educate" the public about the promise of the nuclear age in a widely publicized 1954 speech before the National Association of Science Writers in which he predicted, "Transmutation of the elements - unlimited power...these and a host of other results all in fifteen years. It is not too much to expect that our children will enjoy in their homes electrical energy too cheap to meter, will know of great periodic regional famines in the world only as a matter of history, will travel effortlessly over the seas and under them and through the air with a minimum of danger and great speeds and will experience a life span far longer than ours..."[6]

These inspirational rantings by the man charged with regulating, as well as developing, nuclear power would not have turned the trick of changing commercial nuclear energy from an illusive promise into reality if they weren't accompanied by a series of more tangible incentives. These included the AEC offer to subsidize much of the early costs of commercialization. Not only would most of the needed research continue to be done at public expense but also fuel was manufactured and supplied at bargain prices and in 1956 the AEC promised to buy the plutonium produced by commercial power plants for the production of nuclear warheads.[7] A final obstacle was removed when Congress passed the Price-Anderson Act in 1957 which severely limited the liability of private developers for damages caused by a nuclear accident, effectively repealing the citizen's common-law right to sue the negligent parties for just compensation.[8]

Although the 1954 Atomic Energy Act did require the AEC to adopt regulations governing the industry, the scope of the regulatory mandate was left entirely vague. This opened the door for Strauss and his supporters to pursue a policy that would essentially permit the industry to regulate itself. In Strauss' words, "The AEC's objective in the formulation of the regulations was to minimize government control of competitive enterprise."[9]

Thus was begun a partnership between private enterprise and government in which the obligation to protect the public interest became an obstacle to the commitment they had made to the rapid development of this high risk industry. The ability of federal regulatory officials to adopt a myopic view that permitted a continual underestimation of the risks inherent in nuclear power is not surprising in that it can be considered an extension of the initial lack of adequate concern by the AEC for the public health effects of the above-ground testing of nuclear weapons. (It took considerable effort by many independent scientists to convince the regulators that nuclear fallout was a serious danger despite repeated AEC assertions to the contrary).[10] Evidence of malfeasance on the part of federal and industry officials during the three decade history of commercial atomic power extends far beyond simple myopia.

The AEC staff, under Strauss, was directed not to promulgate strict safety regulations that might restrain industry nor to initiate the much needed research without which there could be no clear understanding of the safety standards required to protect the public.[11] The AEC engaged in an extensive public relations campaign along with the Atomic Industrial Forum (an industry lobbying group) which included the production and distribution of films that presented an exaggerated picture of the benefits of nuclear energy with no hint of the serious potential hazards that the AEC had been warned about by its scientific advisors.[12]

Spurred on by the generous economic incentives and favorable regulatory climate offered by the federal government, the fledgling nuclear industry was able to persuade the utilities to begin ordering nuclear power stations to produce electrical power. The strategy of such industry giants as General Electric and Westinghouse was to offer their initial nuclear power plants at below the actual cost in order to entice the utilities and gain acceptance and a competitive advantage in the nuclear marketplace.[13] Although such a "loss leader" strategy is an accepted practice among detergent producers, soft drink manufacturers and supermarket managers, it is at best questionable whether it was ethical to get regulated utility monopolies hooked on nuclear power through deceptive pricing. It can be argued that today's consumers who face huge electric rate increases due to nuclear power plants with cost overruns in excess of 1,000%, might be justified in laying a large fraction of the blame for their predicament on such early industry policies.

It has been pointed out in a study by energy economist, Charles Komanoff, that deceptive economic practices on the part of the nuclear industry did not end with the acceptance of nuclear power by utility planners.[14] Komanoff demonstrated how the Atomic Industrial Forum used biased methods in its much quoted annual survey of electric generating costs to calculate a 1.5¢ per kilowatt hour cost for nuclear plants in 1978 compared to 2.3¢ KWH for coal plants. When the biases were removed, the relative costs were reversed.

The extent to which the AEC was willing to go to prevent the public from learning about the potential hazards of nuclear power was revealed in a *New York Times* front page story on Nov. 10, 1974.[15] According to the report, AEC documents revealed repeated efforts by the Commission over a ten-year period to suppress studies by its own scientists who found nuclear reactors to be more hazardous than the AEC officially acknowledged and who raised new questions about safety devices. In addition, the documents confirmed charges by nuclear critics that the AEC ignored recommendations from its consultants that research be done on vital safety questions. The most extensively documented case of information suppression described in the report is the case of the study referred to as "WASH-740 revision" which involved an effort by Brookhaven National Laboratories to update a previous assessment of the estimated damages from a major reactor failure. When this study concluded that a worst case accident could affect an area as large as the State of Pennsylvania and cause ten times the deaths, injuries and damages previously estimated, AEC officials made the conscious decision not to make these results public. The details of this particular cover-up and of numerous other highly questionable actions on the part of the AEC with respect to the entire safety issue have been well documented in several books critical of the nuclear industry.[16]

The *New York Times* article also reported that the AEC had consulted with nuclear industry officials on at least two important matters before deciding not to publish studies critical of its safety procedures. This added to a growing chorus of complaints about the interconnections between the AEC and the industry it was supposed to regulate. In an effort to satisfy the many critics of Federal nuclear policy who had focused on the inherent conflict between the AEC roles as promoter and regulator of atomic energy, Congress passed an Energy Reorganization Act in 1974.[17] The AEC was abolished and a new agency, the Nuclear Regulatory Commission(NRC), was established and charged only with the safety responsibilities. The promotional role was assigned to the new Energy Research and Development Agency, which was the forerunner of the subsequently established Department of Energy.

The history of the NRC reveals that the effects of the 1974 reorganization were little more than cosmetic.[18] For the most part, the new

NRC posts were filled by former AEC officials. Not only were the actors the same, but they continued to play similar roles ignoring recommendations for further safety studies, suppressing reports that might alarm the public and maintaining their cozy relationships with leaders of the industry they were supposed to regulate.

The Three Mile Island accident, which occurred in March of 1979 produced a flurry of investigations and criticisms of the NRC and the nuclear industry. A Senate inquiry revealed that the NRC press releases had misled the public and the White House during the accident.[19] The General Accounting Office once again raised questions about the conflicts between the promotional and regulatory activities of the federal government in a report that revealed that virtually all of the outside research for the NRC was done by the Department of Energy.[20] In response to the new round of criticism, the NRC developed a Three Mile Island Action Plan. In the judgement of nuclear critics, such as Daniel Ford of the Union of Concerned Scientists, the implementation of this Action Plan resulted in some "inexpensive 'quick fixes' rather than major, long-term safety improvements."[21] The changes made in the staff and organization of the NRC by President Carter after the T.M.I. accident in order to restore confidence in its regulatory ability have been more than undone by the single-mindedly pronuclear and uncritical attitude of the nuclear officials appointed under the Reagan administration.

Inappropriate governmental activities in support of nuclear power have not been confined to the AEC and the NRC. A Comptroller General Report to Congress concluded that in early 1976 the Energy Research and Development Agency attempted to influence the outcome of a vote in California on a Nuclear Safeguards Initiative by releasing 78,600 copies of a heavily biased report entitled "Shedding Light on Facts About Nuclear Energy."[22] The Central Intelligence Agency made its pronuclear contribution by covering up information it had uncovered about a major nuclear accident in the Soviet Union which was subsequently discovered as a result of a Freedom of Information Act request.[23]

The magnitude of the perhaps less surprising, but equally distressing efforts of the nuclear fuel and equipment manufacturers, the utilities and their powerful financial backers cannot be thoroughly covered within the confines of this essay. The pervasive efforts of the coalition of interests often referred to as the "Atomic Industrial Complex" to overwhelm the public with pro-nuclear propaganda has been described and documented by the authors of several critiques of the industry.[24] The media publicity accorded to the circumstances surrounding the death in 1974 of Karen Silkwood, an employee of the Kerr-McGee Corporation's nuclear fuel plant,[25] raised national consciousness about the potential threats to the public resulting from lax standards and illegal activity within the nuclear industry. At the time she died in an automobile crash, Ms. Silkwood was on her way to deliver documents to a *New York Times* reporter that she and the Oil Chemical and Atomic Workers (OCAW) Union (which represented Kerr McGee's employees) alleged were proof of serious health and safety violations. Although the documents mysteriously disappeared from the crash scene and have never been found, subsequent investigations by the NRC and other governmental agencies substantiated most of the Union's allegations.[26] The mistrust of the nuclear industry and its federal regulators is such that the results of official inquiries which concluded that Ms. Silkwood's death was accidental have done little to convince OCAW officials and others familiar with the case that she wasn't the victim of foul play.

Attempts by government and private enterprise to deal with the many forms of hazardous radioactive waste produced in nuclear power plants, and during all phases of the nuclear fuel cycle, have been researched and chronicled in great detail in a book by journalist Fred Shapiro.[27] The ongoing efforts to find a permanent, environmentally acceptable solution to the radwaste problem has been characterized by the same repeated miscalculations, unjustified public reassurance and lax regulatory control that is manifest in the reactor development program. Included in Shapiro's narrative are descriptions of the widespread contamination of many areas around uranium ore processing plants by dangerous radioactive tailings, the sanctioned use of these tailings in the construction of homes and shopping malls, and the many leaks and other sources of contamination that have occurred in present temporary waste storage facilities. Yet most publicists for, and leaders of the atomic industry, continue to claim that the nuclear waste issue is simply a political controversy and that all of the serious technical questions have been answered.

Alvin Weinberg, one of the leading and most philosophical members of the nuclear establishment, has characterized the decision to develop nuclear power as a "Faustian bargain with society",[28] which requires eternal vigilance on the part of a "nuclear priesthood" to protect the public from the unique hazards of this technology. Weinberg has advocated the development of a new generation of much safer reactors which he considers a necessary and achievable step to regain public confidence by reducing risks to an acceptable level.[29] Denis Hayes, who headed the federal government solar research program during the Carter administration claims that, "Arguments against nuclear power are rooted in a simple paradox. Commercial nuclear power is viable only under social conditions of absolute stability and predictability. Yet the mere existence of fissile materials undermines the security that nuclear technology requires."[30] Given the realities of the present state of our society and the world, Hayes rejects the possibility of achieving a sufficiently safe and secure nuclear energy system.

Acceptance of either the Weinberg or Hayes positions on the viability of safe commercial nuclear power should not be a determining factor in judging the ethical standards that have prevailed to date among those responsible for developing and regulating this industry. It is hard for this author to imagine that anyone researching the history of entanglements between public officials and private interests that continue to dominate this enterprise could fail to conclude that those involved have frequently ventured outside the bounds of acceptable behavior. It is in the clear interest of anyone who recognizes the complexity of the problem of containing the unique potential health hazards intrinsic to nuclear power production to demand a much higher standard of behavior from those entrusted with this awesome task.

ADDENDUM

The foregoing text was written before the disastrous explosion in April of 1986 at the Chernobyl nuclear plant, 60 miles north of Kiev in the Soviet Union. The shock of this first unequivocal demonstration of the enormity of the potential devastation inherent in the commercial development of nuclear energy raised new doubts around the world about the future of this technology.[31] Both the Nuclear Regulatory Commission and the nuclear industry responded by making every effort to draw distinctions between the inherently less safe graphite-moderated Soviet reactors and the more stable light water designs that characterize all commercial U.S. reactors. Although the press gave ample coverage to the 31 immediate Chernobyl fatalities, less attention was paid to the additional worldwide cancer deaths that might ultimately result from radiation exposure, which some experts predicted would be in the tens of thousands.

As the increased fear of nuclear power attributable to Chernobyl has begun to wane, advocates of fission power have seized upon the growing concern about predictions of global warming to promote their cause. They point out that unlike other energy technologies, the nuclear option does not result in the emission of gasses that contribute to the "greenhouse effect," or to the production of acid rain. There have been some optimistic recent predictions of a revival of the nuclear industry, with renewed interest in reactor designs that are claimed to be inherently safer.[32-33] But other experts are not persuaded that nuclear energy is likely to prevent globalwarming.[34-35]

The Reagan administration did not join the leaders of several other industrial countries who responded to Chernobyl by reducing their commitments to nuclear power. After a brief review, the NRC concluded that no fundamental changes were called for in U.S. nuclear technology. The Department of Energy continued to spend a major fraction of its research and development dollars on nuclear fission. Despite this favored treatment, the nuclear industry remained in a moribund state with not a single electric power utility being persuaded to order a new nuclear plant. The strength of public opposition to and distrust of the industry resulted in a decision by the governor of New York to successfully block the opening of the completed Shoreham nuclear plant on Long Island.

The Bush administration is continuing where Reagan left off. The energy plan being presented to Congress once again includes proposals that are intended to stimulate a rebirth of interest in nuclear energy. Rather than respond to distrust by strengthening the review process and making it more independent of the nuclear industry, the President has chosen a strategy that is likely to make the public even more wary. The plan calls for a significant reduction in the opportunity to question and challenge plans for new nuclear facilities. It seems unlikely that this brute force approach will prove acceptable to legislators who know that their constituents would not be pleased to have a technology that they fear forced down their throats.

NOTES

[1]B. Commoner, *The Poverty of Power*, Alfred Knopf, New York (1976), Pp. 76, 77.

[2]R. Nader and J. Abbotts, *The Menace of Atomic Energy*, W. W. Norton, New York (1979) Pg. 26.

[3]M. C. Olson, *Unacceptable Risk*, Bantam Book, New York (1976), Pg. 53.

[4]The early history of nuclear power development and the lack of regulatory diligence on the part of the AEC are well documented in Daniel Ford's acclaimed book *The Cult of the Atom — The Secret Papers of the Atomic Energy Commission*, Simon and Schuster, New York (1982).

[5]D. Ford, *The Cult of the Atom*, Simon and Schuster, New York (1982) Pg. 46.

[6]Ibid., Pg. 50.

[7]Reference 3, Pg. 54.

[8]Reference 5, Pg. 45.

[9]Ibid., Pp. 50-53.

[10]B. Commoner, *The Closing Circle*, Alfred Knopf, New York (1971), Chapt. 3.

[11]Reference 5, Pg. 53.

[12]Ibid., Pg. 48.

[13]I. C. Bupp et. al., "The Economics of Nuclear Power", *Technology Review*, February 1975, Pg. 15.

[14]C. Komanoff, "Power Propaganda", Environmental Action Foundation, March 1980.

[15]D. Burnham, "AEC Files Show Effort to Conceal Safety Perils", *The New York Times*, Nov. 10, 1974, Pg. 1.

[16]See, for example: Reference 5, Pp. 46-166 and Reference 2, Pp. 261-310.

[17]Reference 5, Pg. 166.

[18]Reference 5, Pp. 213-234.

[19]*The New York Times*, "Senate Inquiry Says Atom Agency Misled Public on Three Mile Island", October 3, 1979.

[20]*The New York Times*, "Nuclear Regulators Using Energy Department Labs", March 8, 1979.

[21]Reference 5, Pg. 234.

[22]Comptroller General, Report to Congress, EMD-76-12, General Accounting Office, Washington D.C.,1976.

[23]Z. A. Medvedev, *Nuclear Disaster in the Urals*, W. W. Norton, New York (1979).

[24]See, for example: J. J. Berger, *Nuclear Power-The Unviable Option*, Ramparts Press, Palo Alto, California, (1976) Chapter 8 and K. Grossman, *Cover-Up : What You Are Not Supposed to Know About Nuclear Power*, The Permanent Press, Sagaponack, New York (1980) Chapter 7.

[25]B. J. Phillips, "The Case of Karen Silkwood", *Ms. Magazine*, April 1975, Pp. 59-66.

[26]Reference 2, Pp. 165-172.

[27]F. Shapiro, *Radwaste: A Reporter's Investigation of Nuclear Waste Disposal*, Random House, New York (1981).

[28]A. Weinberg, "Social Institutions and Nuclear Energy", *Science*, July 7, 1972, Pp. 27-34.

[29]A. Weinberg, "Is Nuclear Energy Necessary?", *The Bulletin of the Atomic Scientists*, March 1980, Pp. 31-35.

[30]D. Hayes, "Nuclear Power : The Fifth Horseman", *Worldwatch Paper 6*, May 1976.

[31]C. Hohenemser and O. Renn, "Chernobyl's Other Legacy," *Environment*, April 1988, Pp. 5-45.

[32]J. de La Ferte, "What Future for Nuclear Power," *The OECD Observer*, April/May 1990, Pp. 26-30.

[33]F. Meeks and J. Drummond, "The Greenest Form of Power," *Forbes*, June 11, 1990, Pp. 116-120.

[34]W. Lanouette, "Greenhouse Scare Reheats Nuclear Debate," *Bulletin Atomic Scientists*, April 1990, 34-37.

[35]A. Miller and I. Mintzer, "Global Warming: No Nuclear Quick Fix," *Bulletin Atomic Scientists*, June 1990, 31-36.

NUCLEAR ENERGY AND ENVIRONMENTAL ETHICS

By Jeff Kluewer
Suffolk Community College

Since I only had a general idea of what the other panelists would say today, I interpreted the role of Commentator rather loosely and prepared some remarks in advance as the "designated humanist" in the discussion.

First of all, nuclear power is not "safe". I would have thought that that was a non-controversial statement at this point. It is dangerous. That is why a radioactive core is placed behind several feet of concrete, beneath several feet of water, why there are hot suits and remote control machinery, emergency systems and evacuation plans. It is arguably the most dangerous industrial activity that humans have ever attempted.

There are many ethical questions raised by nuclear power; I'll try to focus on three:

1.   Should we accept the risks of catastrophe that come with nuclear power plants, whatever the probability that they will ever occur?

2.   Should we accept routine and continuous radiation releases from the nuclear fuel cycle?

103

3. Should we accept the eternal toxins generated by the nuclear fuel cycle?

I should stop to say that while I am pleased to be addressing a conference of diverse professionals on nuclear ethics, there seems to be, unfortunately, a clear and extreme inverse proportion between the urgency of ethical concerns and the probability of their influencing public policy. For example, these three ethical issues are specifically forbidden to be raised at federal nuclear power plant licensing hearings. One can question if a plant follows its design, but not if the design will actually prevent or control an accident. One cannot question the amount or consequences of routine radioactive releases, either at the nuclear power plant or along the fuel cycle that supports it. Nor may one ask what is to be done with 20 or 30 or 40 years worth of extremely dangerous radioactive waste generated by the plant.

But we *can* talk. You have already heard "probability risk assessment" discussed. Let me add that nuclear power is a young technology. Only two reactors have operated for more than 20 years and those are very small by today's standards (72 megawatts and 185 megawatts). Only three reactors larger than 1000 megawatts have operated more than 10 years. There is currently too little information to say for certain just how accident-prone large nuclear plants will become with age. Given variations in reactor size, type, and manufacturer, the confident assurance of hundreds of "reactor-years" of experience does not really stand for much. Indeed, given that nuclear power has been introduced and developed to its current state with so little prior full-scale testing and so much retrofitted modification, it is fair still to call it experimental. There are thousands of reportable "events" every year, many serious, many involving radiation releases.[1] These releases are called safe by the government and little is done to prevent recurrences. In this system major accidents become research opportunities used to prove that the technology is working. This official complacency has already contributed to the three most serious commercial accidents in the United States: the partial meltdown of the Fermi fast breeder reactor near Detroit in 1966; the disabling of two reactors at Brown's Ferry in Alabama in 1975; and the partial meltdown at Three Mile Island in 1979.

But even given a more conscientious Nuclear Regulatory Commission, the outlook is not bright.

In November, 1984 the Advisory Committee on Reactor Safeguards was forced to tell NRC Commissioner James Asselstine that "the probability of a core-degrading accident between now and the end of the century may lie in the neighborhood of one in ten..."[2]

Charles Perrow in his new book *Normal Accidents*, which investigates what he calls the unavoidable danger of the "system accident" and which uses nuclear power plants as a prime negative example, notes that the nuclear industry had but 35 "reactor-years" of experience with the size and type of reactor that failed at Three Mile Island, "infancy" for a system so large and complex. Because of the "interactive complexity" of nuclear plants and their "tight coupling" of events and consequences, he expects an accident worse than Three Mile Island within 10 years.[3]

Perrow, among others, discounts the usefulness of so-called quantifiable probability risk assessment and its practitioners who chide the public for accepting highway and smoking deaths, but protesting nuclear power ones. He sees instead a "social rationality" in those who would avoid risks seen as "involuntary, delayed, unknown, uncontrollable, unfamiliar, catastrophic, dreaded, and fatal."[4] The probability risk assessors who see no distinction between 45,000 dispersed highway fatalities and the 45,000 immediate deaths predicted in the updated Brookhaven National Laboratory WASH-740 study of reactor accident consequences earn Perrow's scorn as practitioners of a "new alchemy where body counting replaces social and cultural values."[5]

It is well to remember that the supposed objective quantification of risks does not provide us with ethical imperatives. The technical issue of defining a risk tells us nothing about whether the risk should be taken. There is no morality or logic in using automobile or industrial accidents, cancer deaths, or background radiation levels as standards for what is allowable or desirable in the nuclear industry. This is to substitute science (even assuming it is accurate science) for ethics; it is to be guilty of G.E. Moore's "naturalistic fallacy"; and it is to confuse what exists in one area with what ought to be in another. Such questionable moral and logical positions derive from a mind-set of technological arrogance and optimism. What science can do, it should do, this mind-set argues, or, in the words of the 1933 Chicago World's Fair guidebook, "Science finds, industry applies, man conforms."

But humans cannot conform to nuclear technology and should not be made to do so. The technology is being given human rights: it is innocent, we say, until proven guilty. A more rational and ethical society might demand that the technology and its fuel cycle be proven safe and manageable before being utilized; but in our society it is difficult to escape the conclusion that its' survival is being judged more important than ours. Time and again the government and industry have demonstrated they prefer economic expediency and utility protection to equity and due process for individuals. This is the conclusion of K. S. Shrader-Frechette's *Nuclear Power and Public Policy: The Social and Ethical Problems of Fission Technology*, the only book length philosophical study of the ethics of nuclear technology I know of.[6]

Routine radioactive releases cause cancers, genetic disease, and the premature diseases of aging, among other consequences. Here is how Shrader-Frechette deals with one NRC regulation concerning these releases which provides that utilities must control emissions if there is a "favorable cost- benefit analysis"; that is, they must control releases so long as it costs them less than $1000 to avoid one "man-rem" of exposure.

According to government calculations, every rad of radiation causes 0.002 genetic deaths among offspring of irradiated ancestors. This means, for example, that in the 30-year lifetime of a particular reactor, if 100 persons in the environs of the plant annually receive the maximum permissible annual dose of low-level radiation (0.5 rem), then this exposure alone will cause at least three of them to produce children who will die from genetic disorders. On the basis of the $1000 per man-rem criterion, these genetic deaths would be allowable, provided that it would cost the utility more than $50,000 to contain the population exposure of 50 man-rems per year. Hence the implicit ethical assumption, underlying the price affixed to radiation pollution controls, is that the deaths of these three children ought to be avoided if it would cost $50,000 or less to do so, but that the deaths are morally acceptable if the cost of preventing them is greater than $50,000. Therefore, the worth of a child's life is assumed to be approximately $17,000.[7]

Other corruptions in this system, in my mind, concern first the self-policing of nuclear construction, which inevitably makes accidents and unplanned releases more frequent when standards are not met, and second the suppression of data which would make the true costs of nuclear electricity more apparent. The suppression of data is accomplished by the self-monitoring of nuclear power plants by the utilities that own, run, and depend on them; by the refusal to monitor or study those affected by the industry, including nuclear workers, especially temporary ones; even the Three Mile Island accident consequences appear to have been neglected by official inquiry; and by the firing of scientists from research projects producing data embarrassing to the industry. Thus the government persists in its decision to impose nuclear technology while suppressing or refusing to research the health consequences of that decision.[8]

The issue of radioactive wastes poses an ultimate ethical barrier to nuclear development. We speak of a nuclear fuel "cycle", but there is none. The system is constipated and backed up: Reactors store spent fuel in limited and temporary spaces. High- and low-level wastes that have made it to waste storage sites are leaking into the environment. Reprocessing nuclear fuel has been a failure and there is no plan for the safe isolation of wastes already generated and the more to come.

Commercial reactor wastes already equal in toxicity, though not in volume, military wastes. Initially the hazard is provided by radioactive fission products. After 800 years the toxicity diminishes to about 50 times that of uranium ore. Thereafter it is the transuranics and their "decay daughters" which pose the biological hazard. They remain thousands of times more toxic than uranium ore for most of 4 million years. What will we do with such material? How can we justify sending such an inheritance into the future? How can we pretend to devise ways to contain this hazard across what are geologic time periods?[9]

An answer was provided by Alvin Weinberg when he was director of the Oak Ridge National Laboratory in 1973. He recommended a "nuclear priesthood" for nuclear power to go along with the military priesthood that watches over nuclear weapons:

[N]o government has lasted continuously for 1,000 years: only the Catholic Church has survived more or less continuously for 2,000 years or so. Our commitment to nuclear energy is assumed to last in perpetuity — can we think of a national entity that possesses the resiliency to remain alive for even a single half-life of plutonium-239? A permanent cadre of experts that will retain its continuity over immensely long times hardly seems feasible if the cadre is a national body.... The Catholic Church is the best example of what I have in mind: a central authority that proclaims and to a degree enforces doctrine, maintains its own long-term social stability, and has connections to every country's own Catholic Church.[10]

Weinberg's fantasy of a priesthood is psychologically revealing, but the notion of a commitment in perpetuity to a course so dangerous with so little knowledge of successful controls and ultimate consequences seems to me an ethical outrage.

The development of nuclear power has been undertaken without the consent or even the knowledge of most people. In all countries it has been imposed in authoritarian, anti-democratic, anti-intellectual, indeed even intellectually dishonest ways. The histories of nuclear technology detail the degree to which secrecy, manipulated information, lying, firings and threats, quasi-religious justifications, and paramilitary controls have been and still are part of the price we are being asked to pay for the "peaceful atom".[11]

We ought to ask for what benefit these limits on human freedom are being imposed. It is a question Kemeny Commission member Carolyn Lewis asked during the presidential inquiry into the accident at Three Mile Island. During a heated debate on the future of nuclear power and responding to a suggestion for an "iron fist" nuclear system, Lewis asked:

I mean we're really saying we're willing to risk health and safety, a serious potential accident, to centralize a source of power with a military type of group... And we're deciding to do all these things for what? We haven't explored whether there are alternatives to getting ourselves electricity.[12]

Nuclear power might be defensible were the alternative mass starvation or some other massive dislocation. But we are talking about an energy form that today contributes only a little more than 10% of our electricity in a system with a nationwide over-capacity of 40% and only about 3% of our total energy consumption; it was only recently that nuclear power passed firewood in its contribution to total energy use. Nuclear power is the most expensive way yet devised to generate electricity and is based on a scarce, non-renewable fuel. The calls to overcome this last defect by use of the

Liquid Metal Fast Breeder reactor run on reprocessed fuel in a plutonium economy, even when proposed with charming appeals to Yankee thrift, should not distract us from the facts that the breeder is many times more dangerous than conventional fission technology. It is interactively more complex, faster (more tightly coupled), and has an even higher potential for catastrophe. It uses molten sodium which must be isolated from both air and water to prevent combustion and explosion, has the capacity for nuclear and not just steam explosions, and relies on massive production and reprocessing of plutonium-239, perhaps the most potent respiratory carcinogen we know, whose toxic life extends 10 to 20 times beyond its 24,000 year half-life.

Over and against this hard future is a developing environmental ethic that stresses the inter-relatedness of human action, technological humility instead of arrogance, and the limits to supply and consumption. This ethic chooses the individual over the machine and the system and chooses principles of equity over utility. It finds the consumption of 30% of the earth's resources by 6% of the world's population, roughly the situation in the United States today, ethically indefensible. It would replace standards of control, exploitation and greed with standards of nurture and stewardship in regard to the earth's resources. It strives to find the sustainable carrying capacity of natural systems and asks how much can be produced dependably for an indefinite period; that is, what can be taken from it without diminishing it so that our endowment to posterity is not a landscape of leaking toxic waste dumps and rising cancer, genetic, and other disease rates.

As a last word to philosophers: A "Viewpoints" piece in last week's *Newsday*[13] noted that philosophers were now interning in Congress under an American Philosophical Association program and it identified two basic approaches to these assignments being taken by the philospher/interns. One approach holds that the contribution of the philosopher is not to come up with answers, but to make clear issues and alternatives. The second approach holds that having made the issues and alternatives clear, it is not inconsistent for a philosopher to pick one value over another. I am more in sympathy with the second approach and, as is obvious, feel that the historical and systems analyses in the studies I have mentioned, as well as several environmental ethics analyses,[14] lead to the same conclusion: that there is a moral imperative to abandon nuclear power for electrical energy production.

If, like philosopher number one, you are not ready to take sides and say where the truth lies, you must at least be ready to give students the intellectual tools to see where it doesn't lie. I mean to refer here to the dependence of ethics on epistemology. While I have no more time to rehearse the details here now, if you believe that nothing died at Three Mile Island, please read the relevant chapters of Wasserman and Solomon's *Killing Our Own* which details how the *New York Times* treated the story of animal and infant deaths and of infant hypothyroidism in the areas around Three Mile Island in the months following the accident.[15] I would recommend to you books like Howard Kahane's *Logic and Contemporary Rhetoric*, subtitled *The Use of Reason in Everyday Life*, as an excellent tool for raising in classrooms the issues surrounding the epistemics of mass communications. We cannot hope for a persuasive environmental ethics if we view uncritically the verbal and visual imagery of the mass communications industry, so tied up itself, economically and in assumptions, with the more destructive activities I associate with nuclear power.

Note: *The figures given here were accurate at the time this paper was delivered. It was not possible for the author to update all the information for its publication in the current volume. But the thrust of the argument remains the same today.*

NOTES

[1]The organization Public Citizen monitors Nuclear Regulatory Commission plant accident reports and publishes a summary and analysis yearly. They are available from the Critical Mass Energy Project, 215 Pennsylvania Avenue, S.E., Washington, D.C. 20003, (202) 546-4996.

[2]Letter to James K. Asselstine, Commissioner, U.S. Nuclear Regulatory Commission, from David A. Ward, Acting Chairman, Advisory Committee on Reactor Safeguards, U.S. Nuclear Regulatory Commission, November 6, 1984, page 3. Ward also writes that "the operational utility of any subjectively generated phrase such as, 'somewhat unlikely' or 'not unlikely' is limited." Nevertheless, Ward suggests that a one-in-ten probability might be characterized as "unlikely" or "not highly likely."

[3]Charles Perrow, *Normal Accidents: Living with High-Risk Technologies* (New York: Basic Books, 1984). Perrow devotes an entire chapter to explaining these terms; we can only note a few summary definitions: "Complex interactions are those of unfamiliar sequences or unplanned and unexpected sequences, and either not visible or not immediately comprehensible" (p. 78). "[T]ight coupling is a mechanical term meaning there is no slack or buffer or give between two items. What happens in one directly affects what happens in the other" (pp. 89-90). The simultaneous presence of these two characteristics produces a new sort of accident potential, "interactive complexity in the presence of tight coupling, producing a system accident. We have produced designs so complicated that we cannot anticipate all the possible interactions of the inevitable failures; we add safety devices that are deceived or avoided or defeated by hidden paths in the systems" (p. 11). In complex modern systems, failure is inevitable and the ability of the system to recover from the failure is limited. [This lack of resilience is also a focus of the excellent analysis of U.S. energy systems by Amory and L. Hunter Lovins in their *Brittle Power* (Andover, Massachusetts: Brick House, 1982).] Perrow's prediction of a nuclear plant meltdown with a release of radioactive materials to the environment is explained and defended in Chapter 2.

[4]Perrow, *Normal Accidents*, 325.

[5]Ibid., 12.

111

[6]K.S. Shrader-Frechette, *Nuclear Power and Public Policy: The Social and Ethical Problems of Fission Technology* (Boston: D. Reidel, 1980).

[7]Ibid., 115-116.

[8]Issues of self-regulation and self-monitoring in the nuclear industry are discusssed in the Union of Concerned Scientists Report *Safety Second: A Critical Evaluation of the NRC's First Decade* (Cambridge, Mass.: UCS, 1985). A history of discrediting of data unfavorable to the nuclear industry and of the scientists producing such data is given in *Nukespeak, The Selling of Nuclear Technology in America* by Stephen Hilgartner, Richard C. Bell, and Rory O'Connor (San Francisco: Sierra Club, 1982). A history of the official responses to issues of radiation and health is given in *Killing Our Own* by Harvey Wasserman and Norman Solomon with Robert Alvarez and Eleanor Walters (New York: Delacorte, 1982).

[9]On radioactive waste, see Donald L. Barlett and James B. Steele, *Forevermore, Nuclear Waste in America* (New York: Norton, 1985).

[10]Quoted in Hilgartner, et al. *Nukespeak*, 58.

[11]Other useful histories of nuclear technology besides those given in note 8 include: Irvin C. Bupp and Jean-Claude Derian, *Light Water, the Nuclear Dream Dissolved* (New York: Basic Books, 1978) and Daniel Ford, *Cult of the Atom* (New York: Simon and Schuster, 1982).

[12]Quoted in Perrow, *Normal Accidents*, 337-338.

[13]William Triplett, "I Think, Therefore I Legislate," *Newsday* April 5, 1985, p. 63.

[14]There are many authors to choose from on this point, but I wish to urge readers to find a most humane and overlooked book by Wendell Berry, *The Unsettling of America, Culture and Agriculture* (San Francisco: Sierra Club, 1977).

[15]Wasserman and Solomon, *Killing Our Own*, chapters 13 and 14.

ENVIRONMENTAL ACTION: LONG ISLAND WATER

By R. E. Watson
Brookhaven National Laboratory

I. Introduction

In this paper we will consider some of the complexities underlying environmental policy and action. Policies associated with the waters of Long Island will be used as the example. The reader will, I hope, find the discussion relevant to environmental issues other than water and to regions other than Long Island. I will not attempt to "solve" Long Island's water problems here, though some factors which I believe to be important to such a solution will be suggested in the discussion.

Two assumptions underlie this essay. The first is the right to, and the necessity for having, potable water. The second is the necessity to preserve our marshes, bays and streams. This second assumption can be argued on several grounds. The wetlands are habitat for a wide variety of species and it may be argued, as was done in earlier sessions of this symposium, that these species have legal and moral rights. The issue may also be argued selfishly, for the terrain in question is important to the food chain, an acre of coastal marsh being more productive than an acre of prime farmland. Granted the needs for both potable water and the preservation of wetlands

113

one immediately encounters a dilemna. The prime recharge area important to Long Island groundwater is the center of the Island. The wetlands and bays, on the other hand, are in a different region, namely along the coast, and public policy which acts to reduce the effects of man's activities in one region will automatically tend to increase man's impact on the other — a garbage dump which is well outside the prime recharge area is inevitably not far from one of the shores. As is often the case, there may be trade-offs in environmental benefits.

Compared with much of the East Coast of the United States, Long Island is doing well in its efforts to preserve potable water. This is due, in part, to planning, in particular to the Long Island Regional Planning Board, which has reduced the ill effects which can follow from unplanned growth. It is also due to some municipalities which have been willing to learn from their, and others, past mistakes. The situation is worse for the wetlands. The coastal zone is either built up or largely mapped for development and the density of such development and its proximity to the wetlands does not bode well. Not all agencies do their jobs well, e.g. Suffolk County, on Long Island, has a mosquito control effort which does mechanical damage to the wetlands, to a degree I believe unnecessary, while endeavoring to combat mosquitoes. Such shortcomings are not limited to the County. The State Department of Environmental Conservation is ineffective. This is partly due to an ever increasing array of mandated duties without the increasing number of employees to deal with them. It is also due to a lack of will in Albany both within and outside of the Department. Mr. Halpin's proposal earlier in this symposium, to separate the conservation and environmental tasks into two separate organizations is an effort to resolve some of DEC's shortcomings. [January 1991: nothing has come of this proposal]

The remainder of this paper will be divided into four parts. The first will deal with scientific "facts" and environmental policy, the second with problems associated with planning and the third with the issue of how the costs of protecting the environment are to be apportioned to different groups in society. The fourth section will deal with the issue of garbage disposal and ground water. This is an issue of primary concern to this writer and provides examples of how legislature oversight can exacerbate problems.

114

II. Scientific "Facts" and Water Preservation

Public officials require facts on which to base environmental policy, particularly if that policy is going to cost the taxpayer money. These facts must satisfy the voter and be able to survive the test of challenge in the courts as well as meeting environmental needs. Technical information does not always fall neatly into this mold. That is, proof scientific is not always the proof necessary for action.

Technical data is often sparse and subject to revision. For example, the "208" study defining Long Island's hydrological zones employed inspired guesswork, when data was lacking, to place the boundaries of the prime recharge area. The boundaries, as drawn, are used as a basis for public policy. In one region, which is subject to heavy municipal and county usage, soil core samples indicate that there should be a significant shift in the boundary, granted the criterion upon which the boundary was originally defined (i.e. which involves the presence of a clay layer separating the surface aquifer from the deep aquifer levels). Such shifts in boundaries prove difficult for public officials to adjust to when they are planning land usage.

Some data is statistical in nature and hard to translate into hard and fast rules for action. This is particularly true when assessing the public health risks associated with levels of pollutants. How much dioxin, heavy metals, or for that matter, lawn fertilizer contaminating ground water is permissible? Some data, if scrutinized, is irrelevant (and yet it may be the only basis we have for justifying a needed course of action).

Meaningful data is often hard to come by and we are often unable to anticipate which environmental factors are, in fact, important. While there is an increasing tendency to preserve the wetlands *per se*, we have a very incomplete understanding of how much and what kind of human activity can occur in the terrain immediately adjacent to wetlands and yet allow them to remain healthy. Technical data, when incompatible with official desires, can be subject to political pressure.

Natural, and imposed factors, important to environmental policy, are sometimes dynamic. As discussed earlier, the hydrological zone boundaries move with changing hydrological conditions. Nature may impose more

115

severe changes: mosquitoes are ineffectively controlled on Long Island (often with unnecessary damage to the wetlands) and there is an uneasy war between those on the South Shore who object to the frequency with which they get bitten and those concerned with damage to the environment. Unfortunately there are a large number of humans living in proximity to a large number of mosquitoes. If and when the mosquitoes become carriers of a serious human disease, public health requirements may lead to action, which, without due care, will devastate the wetlands. This has happened with DDT in the past.

Factors which are ill-defined, often statistical and subject to change are hard for the best intentioned of public officials to translate into public policy.

III. Planning and the Environment

Compared with many of the other areas of the United States which are subject to rapid growth, Long Island has been fortunate in the quality of its regional and municipal planning and in the translation of that planning into action by public officials. Unfortunately there is a lag time between the plan and its effect on public action.

The Long Island regional master plan, drawn up in the 1960's, proposed that the major population and commercial buildup be along a central corridor in the vicinity of the Long Island Expressway and the central railroad line. This plan is reflected in planning practices, in zoning maps and in real estate investments to this day. We now discover that this corridor goes through the centers of the most sensitive hydrological zones. In eastern Long Island this has led to conflicts between the county and municipalities as to who is to control the development which will or will not be allowed. In western Long Island, it is simply declared that there is sufficient water and development goes on unabated. The ideas of twenty years ago are contributing to the problems of today.

Like the rest of us, planners do not always learn from their past mistakes. There is a large sewer district, the Southwest Sewer District, in Suffolk County. It is billed as a water preservation effort by those who wish to sell more sewer systems, but it is more aptly termed a water depletion project because the effluent collected is given primary sewage treatment and then piped out and dumped in the Atlantic Ocean. This is leading to a

116

significant drop in the water table in the region served by the District. A proper terciary treatment of the sewage, followed by recharge into the ground is desirable but the cost to re-engineer and rebuild this system, already plagued by misdesign and excessive costs, is out of the question. Rather than learning lessons from the District's shortcomings our regional planning board is busy searching for more customers for the District and planning more sewer districts without satisfactorily facing the issue of proper recharge to replenish the groundwater.

IV. Who Is To Pay?

Granted that Long Island's aquifers are underground, not like the more familiar surface reservoirs, should there be massive public investment in the recharge area over them? While serious sources of pollution must of course be avoided, the degree to which development should be restricted in the recharge area is unclear. In any case, there is little inclination towards large scale public aquisition of the recharge area.

Should the land owner pay the cost of water protection? The aquifer can be protected, in principal, by reducing the density of usage over it, such as by 5 or 10 acre residential zoning. This is fine for the wealthy but not for those of modest means. Restricting development over an aquifer affects the economy of the surrounding area as well. Should other areas,which continue to grow and which rely on this aquifer as insurance against the depletion of their water, compensate the restricted region for the constraints put on its economy? Further, should these other areas be called upon to restrict any further development which would further degrade the aquifer under them?

The answer to all these questions seems to be: "let the other guy pay." Environmentalists are frequently charged with being elitists: there is some justice in this because it is often those of modest means who are called on to make the greatest sacrifices — such as not being able to find affordable housing.

V. Garbage, Water and Legislative Oversight

In recent years, Long Island has relied primarily on land filling its garbage, but even landfills with protective liners under them have a history of leachate plumes. In response to this threat to the ground water, New

117

York State has mandated that, by 1990, the municipalities on Long Island adopt some other technique as the primary means of garbage disposal, namely incineration. The heat which is produced by this burning may then either be sold or used to generate electricity. At first glance the idea makes considerable sense. However, after having instructed Long Island to spend roughly a billion dollars on such incinerators, the State, through oversight and indifference, has neglected its role in helping make such a system work.

Unfortunately garbage disposal, by any means, tends to pollute and the State's demand to protect groundwater by reduced usage of landfills is done with the probable degradation of the air we breath. The State has yet to define the air standards which the incinerators must meet-it's already late for such standards to be built into the design of a plant to be brought into operation by 1990 (or beyond). Worse, the State has not faced up to the economic and political issues which arise if its air emissions standards prove inadequate in the future, and this will likely be the case. Changes in the air standards (as well as inadequacies of plant design and operation) could lead to expensive retrofitting or even the closure of plants. Insurance to cover this is simply not available to the municipalities and this is, in part, due to the laws of New York State.

The best way to reduce the adverse effects of garbage disposal on our air, ground and water is to reduce the amount of garbage entering the waste stream. This runs counter to some of the most powerful marketplace forces in our society. The second best thing is to reduce the more noxious parts of the waste stream and to recycle what one can. Plastics are high on the list of undesirables for either landfilling or burning. Because of the chemical diversity of the plastics encountered, they are not amenable to recycling, though this may change. Among other items, leaves, brush,glass, paper and metal can be recycled with a significant reduction in the volume of garbage (and a significant improvement in the quality of what remains as an incinerator fuel). However, recycled materials require markets. These markets are sparse and market prices reflect the health of the economy. In the long run, recycling should be one of the cheapest methods of waste disposal, but in the short term, widespread recycling of municipal waste is going to require all the assistance it can get. It may require legislation or subsidies favoring its transportation and usage-or at least the removal of subsidies we now have (such as tax write-offs) favoring virgin materials. Except for a law encouraging the purchase of recycled over

118

virgin paper for state government use, New York has done nothing to define, identify or encourage markets for recycled materials.[1] In contrast, New Jersey has placed a surcharge on other means of waste disposal and the income from this is being used to subsidize the start up of recycling.

Recycling does not represent a "big" solution to our garbage problems and hence it has yet, if ever, to become fashionable. Large incinerators and large sewer districts have their constituencies in the financial institutions which will float the bond issues and in the building trades. Big solutions are often not the best solutions for environmental problems but thinking big is an American tradition.

There are other ways in which government at the federal and state levels might rationally assist municipalities, short of subsidizing them, towards a more economic and less polluting handling of solid and liquid wastes. We will not dwell on these matters here. The point of this section is that the legislative process often fails to face up to the implications of the law being written and, once the law has been written, the problem is presumed to be solved. The New York State law phasing out primary use of landfilling (landfilling is still required for the ash and for that trash which can't be burnt) on Long Island is a good example of this.

ADDENDUM

[January 1991: Some things have changed — The State of New York has accepted recycling as a solution to part of its solid-waste problems, but the State still places major reliance on incinerators. These incincrators have been refined to the point where air emissions have been reduced to reasonable limits. The incinerator ash remains a hazard to landfill because of heavy metals and likelihood that some hydrocarbons, such as PCB's are incompletely burned. In the last half year, the DEC has allowed municipalities to consider alternate technologies, such as the composting of municipal waste. What is unchanged is that the State has done little to assist the process (such as encouraging recycling industries) or to reduce the hazards (such as a household battery return law, thus keeping heavy metals out of the waste stream in the first place) of municipal waste disposal. Our society still prefers "big" solutions to problems even when the "small" would work better.]

VI Conclusion

At its onset, this symposium considered man's relation to his environment in philosophical terms. This relationship was then considered in terms of our courts of law and politics. In the final sessions we have considered two environmental matters of great interest to us on Long Island — nuclear power and water. In my presentation concerning water, I have attempted to indicate some of the difficulties in translating scientific information into environmental action and some of the complexities facing the most well-meaning of public officials when dealing with such matters. As for Long Island water, the public actions, underway these days, should lead to potable, if not exactly pristine, water for most of Long Island for the foreseeable future. This author is less optimistic for the wetlands and the life residing in them: it seems that the pressure of human population in the New York City area and elsewhere, can only lead to substantial damage.

The author is a solid state physicist. He is also on several committees appointed by Brookhaven Town, Suffolk County, Long Island, including ones concerned with the coastal zone and with garbage disposal.

NOTE

[1]There is a one-man recycling office in the New York State DEC, but its efforts are limited to making grants, of up to $25,000, to assist municipalities in acquiring the hardware, such as dumpsters, they need for setting up recycling programs. This is only slightly better than doing nothing at all.

ETHICAL CONCERNS AND ENVIRONMENTAL WATER ISSUES

By Julian Kane
Hofstra University

How do ethics affect environmental issues differently from other societal issues? The effects of dumping toxic wastes into water supplies are orders of magnitude greater than discarding litter in the streets, but the ethics involved are similar. Doing the "right" thing involves a decision not to impose a burden on society and the environment that properly should be dealt with by the individual.

Scientists and engineers employed by industry, water suppliers and governmental agencies are often confronted by ethical problems in taking positions favored by their employers that might be detrimental to the environment. Recommendations contrary to the employers' interests can result in demotion, firing or some other career damage. Some individuals attempt to resolve an ethical dilemma by surreptitiously divulging information to the press or to others who can expose environmental abuses without fear of reprisal. Such a course may be proper depending on the magnitude of the problem.

The following cases show how ethics were involved in varying degrees over the years in Long Island water issues.

123

The 1976 Hudson River Project

When the Army Corps of Engineers proposed that Nassau County be included in their $4.6 billion project to provide New York City and part of Long Island with Hudson River water, Nassau engineers supported the plan which could have allowed accelerated development if Hudson water were available to cover the increased consumption Nassau's urbanization would entail. The project was aborted, however, after major river contamination by PCB's and chemical spills were revealed along with a questionable fiscal arrangement. Nassau withdrew, and the project then collapsed. The County is not involved in the city's present plan to supplement its high quality Catskill water with dubious quality Hudson water by 1995.

Nitrate Standards and Sewering Criteria

In sparsely populated suburban areas where soil permeability enables on-site septic systems to function properly, sewers and sewage treatment plants are not needed. These usually would attract intensive development once they are constructed and result in large-scale water consumption increases due to increased population and to wasteful discharges of treated water effluent from the plants to the sea rather than to the ground where recycling to the aquifers can take place.

The U.S. nitrate standard for drinking water is 10 mg/l, which is twice as restrictive as need be considering that the World Health Organization standard followed by all other industrial nations is 22 mg/l; and considering that methemoglobinemia, the principal nitrate disease, has almost never occurred in U.S. water supplies where nitrates far exceeded the standard.

In 1978, the Long Island Regional Planning Board's epic *208-Wastewater Management Study* recommended sewering in areas were nitrate concentrations were only 6 mg/l; despite data within the report indicating on-site septic systems were responsible for only 27% of the groundwater nitrate burden — with fertilizers being the major source. The recommendation could have enabled nitrates to become a trigger for sewering, but the federal EPA, which funds most sewering projects, was convinced to rule that nitrates would be used only as an indicator of the possible presence of more serious contaminants that would have to be verified prior to sewering.

124

Composting of Industrial-Municipal Sewage Sludge.

In 1980, a Nassau County plan to end ocean discharges of industrial-municipal sludge by substituting composting and use as a soil-additive was endorsed by state and federal authorities who provided $33 million to build the composting facilities. The project would have been implemented despite its hazards to soil, crops, air and ground water if internal county memos had not been surreptitiously obtained and publicized. The county withdrew from the project, and a federal judge compelled a consent decree to be signed permitting marine sludge discharges to continue under the previous regulations until definite proof was available to show it was harmful to the ocean environment.

Although no such evidence of harm specifically attributable to the sludge has ever been found, particularly at the shifted deep-water discharge site more than 120 miles offshore, Congress and the president unanimously passed a new law in 1988 to end marine sludge discharges by 1992 because of the erroneous impression that sludge was involved in the notorious 1988 beach pollution incidents along New Jersey and Long Island shores. The real culprits were garbage, medical wastes, crack needles and raw sewage — with sludge not being involved at all. When ignorance and misconceptions won out over logic and factual evidence, many scientists hesitated to speak up for fear of offending their governmental or industrial superiors who had been involved in the hasty decision to end marine sludge discharges. The present plans to pelletize the municipal sludge for use as fertilizer would jeopardize soils, crops, milk and water supplies with cadmium, lead, mercury and other toxic substances just as the composted industrial-municipal sludge would have. Oceanic dispersion and dilution offer the best environmental solution for the near future, but officials are loathe to admit they were twice wrong, and scientists hesitate to reveal that the emperor has no clothes.

Preservation of the Lloyd Aquifer

In 1981, an application by the Roosevelt Field Water District to tap Long Island's deepest and purest aquifer, the Lloyd, to replace two Magothy aquifer wells lost through contamination was supported by county, state and federal authorities despite the fact that the Lloyd contains less water than the other aquifers and despite its being the only aquifer suitable for use in coastal areas that had experienced saltwater intrusion in the others. A hasty decision to grant the application was overturned when evidence revealed that 50% of the district's warm weather public supply water use was for air conditioning and other nonpotable purposes. The water district could have used nonpotable aquifer water for air conditioning and could have promulgated conservation to reduce usage stress of its remaining potable Magothy wells, but it chose not to do either. Heavy overpumping of its Magothy wells had drawn organic contaminants from past industrial waste discharges into two of its five public supply wells, but with conservation, the remaining Magothy wells were able to meet the district's needs. As a result of this case, the Lloyd aquifer has been designated as an emergency reserve aquifer for future potable use only, except where it is currently being used.

The Manhasset Hydrogeologic Zone Boundary

In 1982, Nassau County consultants recommended shifting a hydrogeologic zone boundary in Manhasset based on new data taken after the boundary had been established. The change could have enabled the Whitney-Payson estate, the largest private holding in the county, to be shifted for developmental purposes from what had been designated as a critical precipitation-recharge area to the public water supply aquifers to a non critical groundwater discharge area to the coastal seas. As such, the property would have been threatened with intensive future development.

The consultants' findings were challenged after details about the methodology were disclosed. They had compared 20 shallow-aquifer pressure readings taken in 1981 with deep-aquifer readings taken in the 1960's. Since this was similar to comparing apples with oranges, the boundary change was put off until contemporaneous deep pressure readings could be taken. When these were found to be lesser than the shallow pressures, the zone boundary remained unchanged and the Whitney-Payson location is still designated as a critical recharge or Special Groundwater Protection Area.

Attempted Sewering in East Hills, L.I.

When extensions of sewage lines were considered in eastern Nassau in 1983, county consultants recommended sewering of developed residential areas where the existing on-site septic systems were functioning properly. Sewering would have allowed large-scale land use and rezoning changes for

126

multistory high-density, residential or commercial uses. When it was divulged that their recommendation was based primarily on analysis of federal soil maps showing the presence of low-permeability clays in the upper five feet of the area, the consultants were requested to make a series of borings to the greater depths at which septic tank leaching pools normally function. After these showed permeable sands to be present, the consultants reversed their recommendation, and the East Hills area involved remains moderate-density residentially zoned and unsewered.

Attempted Sewering in North Hills, L.I.

Until 1985, the policies of Nassau's Health and Public Works Departments called for 100% sewering throughout the entire county; even in little-developed and low-density populated areas where permeable sands enabled on-site septic systems to function satisfactorily. When developers attempted to have county sewer lines extended beyond the existing boundary to serve a future condominium project planned for a North Hills forest area located within a designated Special Groundwater Protection Area, the County Board of Supervisors was convinced to reverse its agencies' policies. The requested sewer line extension was denied on the basis that a legal precedent might be established that would open the floodgates to many other developers who would also seek entry into SGPAs; which could cause significant contamination of the public supply aquifers inasmuch as SGPA precipitation recharge finds its way into the deep groundwater all over the county.

Backflow Contamination of Water Mains

Cross-connections of water lines can allow backflow from buildings into street mains whenever a pressure drop might occur in the mains. One-way valves or controls have been mandated by the N.Y. State Health Department since 1978 for facilities with hazardous substances such as hospitals, medical laboratories and chemical firms from which backflow could introduce toxic substances into the drinking water. Many industries resisted installing the controls and many L.I. water suppliers (with apparent county Health Department concurrence) were reluctant to implement the annual inspection and testing programs involved. An appeal to the State Health Comissioner resulted in action being initiated at the county level, but delays were encountered when the State Public Service Commission refused to allow water service to be shut off to industries that would not allow

Health Department inspection of premises to determine whether piping and control violations existed. Eventually, public pressure and hearings resolved the issue by 1986, and all L.I. water suppliers now have cross- connection programs that held assure a safer quality water supply.

Zoning Density Waivers in Special Groundwater Protection Areas

Article 10 of Nassau's Health Ordinances limits development in SGPAs (undeveloped critical recharge areas to the water supply aquifers) in effect to 0.8 residential units per acre. When a former County Health Commissioner granted developers a waiver of this provision in 1988 that would have enabled a precedent-setting larger number of condominiums per acre to be built on a 65-acre North Hills forested parcel, protests to the County Executive resulted in the retirement of the Commissioner and in the Health Department citing another regulation on waste disposal that has prevented development and destruction of the forest to this day (1991). A particularly vexing aspect of this case was the ex-Commissioner's action in the face of opposition by his five top departmental officials.

Pumping Restrictions in Nassau County

When the State Department of Environmental Conservation imposed pumping limits (caps) on 41 Nassau water suppliers in order to prevent depletion of the potable groundwater resources which increased pumping trends were leading towards, many of the suppliers initially contested the caps. The limits were based on five-year average pumping amounts in each supplier-district that were to be revised as future trends warranted. The caps curtailed expansion by the suppliers and in effect limited development to whatever increased water might become available through conservation. Nassau's largest supplier, the Long Island Water Corporation, went through a costly hearing and court challenge; claiming its increased pumping amounts did not lower the water table or cause saltwater intrusion. It lost all the way through the Appellate Division; largely on the basis of evidence introduced over the corporation's objection, that increased pumping trends in their wells had matched decreased water table heights and increased presence of saltwater. The State was able to show that Brooklyn and western Queens had lost their aquifer water supplies decades earlier due to saltwater intrusion caused by similar over pumping and water table declines. Although one of the smaller suppliers successfully reversed its cap, the precedent of the L.I. Water Corporation defeat in effect has

128

sustained the pumping limits and helped protect against future saltwater intrusion.

Toxic Chlorination Byproducts in Drinking Water

Chlorine added to drinking water as a disinfectant since 1904 has saved millions of lives by preventing cholera, typhoid and other waterborne epidemic diseases, but we have known at least since 1973 that chlorine can cause many other health problems by combining with natural soil compounds in water to form carcinogenic trihalomethanes such as chloroform. Despite this, both the U.S. EPA and the N.Y. State Health Department allow 20 times more trihalomethanes in public water supplies (100 ug/l) than most other toxic organic chemicals (5 ug/l). Water suppliers desiring to continue using chlorine instead of switching to safer but costlier ozone for disinfection have apparently been successful thus far in their lobbying efforts. However, N.Y. State suppliers distributing bacteria-free deep-aquifer groundwater, who have approved cross-connection controls as well as adequate piping, equipment and maintenance procedures, can obtain annually renewable Disinfection Waivers permitting them to eliminate chlorination. Some 470,000 people on Long Island drink nonchlorinated water because their suppliers can meet the higher operational standards needed to get the waivers. Some 2 million other Long Islanders, however, are supplied with the same bacteria-free deep aquifer water that must be chlorinated because their suppliers are unable or refuse to obtain waivers.

With the recent publication of *Water Chlorination* volume 6, 1990 by Jolley et al, there is evidence that as many as 22 individual toxic chlorination byproducts may be reacting synergistically in drinking water to cause the high incidence of chlorination's known association with bladder cancer and with colon cancer deaths. The toxic byproducts of chlorine in drinking water include mutagenic haloacetonitriles, ketones and furanones, neurotoxic haloacid derivatives and fetotoxic chlorophenols in addition to the carcinogenic trihalomethanes. When informed of these latest known hazards of chlorination, of the many Long Island suppliers who chlorinate, the Great Neck North Water Authority broke ranks and announced it would move expeditiously to end chlorination as soon as it had replaced all deficient piping that would enable it to obtain a waiver.

60 Trillion Gallons Is Not an Unlimited Groundwater Resource

A Nassau official declared in 1990 that the county did not have a water quantity problem because its water table decline of several feet since development began in the 1940's represented a mere 0.75% loss of water from the 1,000-foot-thick aquifer system. This reasoning is analogous to that of a speaker at the 1985 Ethics and Environment Conference who contended that water conservation on Long Island was unnecessary because the aquifers contained 60 trillion gallons of fresh water. Such logic which could support unlimited pumping, sewering and development, ignores the fact that Nassau's water table decline of 8.5 feet between the 1940's and the late 1980s actually represents a 14% loss from the 62-foot height of groundwater that existed above sea level in the 1940's. Regardless of what depth the water is pumped from, the greater pressure of a high water table maintains the fresh quality of the entire aquifer thickness by keeping the coastal seawater out. Were excessive pumping allowed to lower the water table to sea level, massive saltwater intrusion would commence as had occurred decades earlier in Brooklyn and western Queens, and the remainder of Nassau's 940 feet of potable groundwater would be rendered useless as a public supply resource. Nassau would not be able to tap into the Catskill reservoir system as Brooklyn and western Queens did, and its entire economic and societal base would be in danger of collapse.

Conclusions

Scientists and engineers may arrive at diametrically opposed positions on environmental issues based on different data, different methodologies, or different interpretations of the same data. Findings and recommendations of scientists and engineers may be influenced by personal considerations or by ethical considerations that value society and the environment as paramount.

Note: Professor Kane was a catalyst who helped shake the established viewpoint in many of these cases.

NOTES ON THE CONTRIBUTORS

ARNOLD BERLEANT is Professor of Philosophy at the C.W. Post Campus of Long Island University. He has taught and published extensively on environment from a philosophical standpoint. A major chapter in his new book, *Art and Engagement* (Temple University Press, 1991) deals with environmental aesthetics, and that discussion will be extended in his forth coming book *Environment and Aesthetics* (Temple).

THEODORE D. GOLDFARB is Associate Professor of Chemistry at the State University of New York at Stony Brook. He received the Ph.D. in physical chemistry from the University of California at Berkeley. His present research, teaching, public service and consulting are in the fields of environmental chemistry and science and public policy with an emphasis on the ecological impacts of alternative energy development strategies, waste management policies and agricultural practices. His publications include an environmental issues reader, an introductory physical science text, and numerous articles in professional journals. He has developed and administered interdisciplinary undergraduate general education and faculty development programs and has taught short courses on energy and environmental issues to high school and college teachers. He received the Chancellor's Award for Excellence in Teaching in 1979 and the NYS/UUP joint Labor-Management Excellence Award in 1990.

PATRICK G. HALPIN was inaugurated as Suffolk County, Long Island's fifth County Executive on January 1, 1988. Halpin assumed the county's highest office after more than a decade in government at the federal, state and county levels. In April of 1982, Halpin was elected to the New York State Assembly where he served until assuming the office of Suffolk County Executive. A staunch environmentalist, Halpin was awarded The Nature Conservancy's 1989 President's Public Service Award for leadership in protecting the county's drinking water supply. A major part of Halpin's comprehensive ground water protection program is acquisition of sensitive pine barrens and conservation of open space. Halpin sponsored the Suffolk County Bottle Law of 1982, and co-sponsored the statewide bill which became law the following year. Under Halpin's direction, the Planning Department is developing a new master plan for the 21st Century to encourage balanced growth. Halpin graduated from Old dominion University in Virginia in 1975 with a Bachelor of Arts degree in government and economics.

RICHARD E. HART, the general editor, is Associate Professor of Philosophy at Bloomfield College, New Jersey and former Executive Committee member of the Long Island Philosophical Society. Dr. Hart was principal organizer and program chair for the LIPS-sponsored conference, Ethics and the Environment, the proceedings of which comprise the present volume. He teaches, and has published widely, in the areas of ethics, social philosophy and philosophy and literature. He serves on the editorial boards of *Metaphilosophy* and *Aitia* and is presently an officer of the American Association of Philosophy Teachers. Dr. Hart's Ph.D. was awarded by the State University of New York at Stony Brook.

JULIAN KANE is Senior Adjunct Professor of Geology at Hofstra University, science teacher at Garden City High and an environmental consultant. He has advised legislative and administrative agencies and citizen groups on environmental, governmental and zoning issues and has authored over 100 publications on water, waste and air quality management — ocean, lunar and planetary matters — and climate, fossils and extinctions. He has received numerous awards from diverse groups such as NASA, the Air Pollution Control Association, the National Association of Conservation Districts, the National Science Teachers Association, the New York Professional Engineers Society and the Nassau County Bar Association.

ERIC KATZ is an assistant professor of philosophy at New Jersey Institute of Technology. He received his Ph.D. in 1983 from Boston University.

His dissertation, *The Moral Justification for Environmentalism,* was the first philosophy dissertation written on the subject of environmental ethics. Katz has published more than a dozen articles in the field, including two annotated bibliographies that appeared in *Research in Philosophy and Technology* (Vol. 9, 1989 and Vol. 12, 1992). He is currently writing a book on "deep ecology." Katz is Vice-President of the International Society for Environmental Ethics. He has presented papers on environmental ethics at universities throughout the United States and Canada, as well as at the United Nations.

JEFF KLUEWER teaches writing, journalism and mass media at Suffolk Community College in Brentwood, New York. He served for many years on the Executive Committee of the Shoreham Opponents Coalition, which successfully opposed the opening of the Shoreham Nuclear Power Station on Long Island. He is currently the editor of the *Rockville Centre Herald.*

CHRISTOPHER P. MOONEY is currently Professor and Chairman of the Philosophy Department at Nassau Community College. He received his B.A. from Columbia University, and his M.A. and Ph.D. from Fordham University. He has published widely on the history and practice of philosophy. One of his major areas of interest is the interface between legal and ethical principles.

EVELYN URBAN SHIRK was educated at Wilson College (A.B.) and Columbia University (M.A., Ph.D.). She is Professor Emeritus of Philosophy at Hofstra University where she taught for forty years, serving as Chair of the Department of Philosophy for over ten years. Her books include *Readings in Philosophy* (co-edited with J. Buchler and J.H. Randall), *Adventurous Idealism: The Philosophy of Alfred Lloyd, The Ethical Dimension,* and *In Pursuit of Awareness* (co-edited with E. Kronevet). She has published articles and reviews in the areas of ethics, aesthetics, philosophy of education and curriculum development, and has, in recent years, developed new and innovative courses in applied ethics, including ethics and technology and environmental ethics.

MICHAEL A. SOUPIOS is an associate professor of Political Science at Long Island University's C.W. Post Campus where he also teaches courses in philosophy. His academic specialties include classical philosophy and modern political theory. Dr. Soupios holds six graduate degrees in areas such as history, political science, philosophy of education and political

133

theory. His publications include a number of articles and reviews on subjects ranging from Platonic philosophy to natural law theory. Dr. Soupios is also the general editor of a volume entitled, *European Political Theory* (UPA, 1986).

DAVID SPRINTZEN is Professor of Philosophy at the C.W. Post Campus of Long Island University. He is the author of *Camus: A Critical Examination* and *The Drama of Thought: An Inquiry Into the Place of Philosophy in Human Experience*. Dr. Sprintzen is a member of The Ethical Humanist Society of Long Island, and has spoken widely on issues concerning the metaphysics of politics and power. He is a founder and long-time chairperson of the Long Island Progressive Coalition, an affiliate of the Citizen Action Network.

ERIC WALTHER is Professor of Philosophy and Computer Science at the C.W. Post Campus of Long Island University. His dissertation was completed at Yale University in 1965 under the direction of Paul Weiss. Current professional interests include Artificial Intelligence, Philosophy of Mind and Philosophy of Science. For several years Dr. Walther has also worked as a construction inspector for Nehemiah Plan Homes, a non-profit affordable housing program for first-time homeowners in Brooklyn, New York.

RICHARD E. WATSON was an undergraduate at Amherst College and obtained a Ph.D. in Physics at MIT. His specialty is the theory of solids and most of his career has been at Brookhaven National Laboratory. He is the recipient of the 1982 Hume-Rothery Award of The Metallurgical Society. He has also been involved in local and municipal affairs and is currently active on Brookhaven Town Committees concerned with county secession, conservation, and solid waste. His participation in the present volume follows from these latter activities.

SELECTED BIBLIOGRAPHY
Environmental Ethics

BOOKS

Allen, Rodney F. et al. *Deciding How To Live On Spaceship Earth:*
The Ethics of Environmental Concern. Winona, Minn: Plover Books,
1973.

Anglemyer, M., Seagraves, E., LeMaistre, C. *A Search For*
Environmental Ethics: An Initial Bibliography. Washington, D.C.:
Smithsonian Press, 1980.

Attfield, Robin. *The Ethics of Environmental Concern,* 2nd ed.
Athens, GA: University of Georgia Press, 1991.

Barbour, Ian G., ed. *Western Man and Environmental Ethics:*
Attitudes Toward Nature and Technology. Reading, MA: Addison-
Wesley Pub. Co., 1973.

Blackstone, W.T. *Philosophy and Environmental Crisis.* Athens, GA:
University of Georgia Press, 1974.

135

Bowman, Douglas C. *Beyond the Modern Mind: The Spiritual and Ethical Challenge of the Environmental Crisis.* New York: Pilgrim Press, 1990.

Cahn, Robert. *Footprints on the Planet: A Search for an Environmental Ethics.* New York: Universe Books, 1978.

Callicott, J. Baird. *In Defense of the Land Ethic: Essays in Environmental Philosophy.* Albany, N.Y.: SUNY Press, 1989.

Cook, Stephen P. *Coming of Age in the Global Village.* Russellville, AR: Parthenon Books, 1990.

Cooper, David E., Palmer, Joy A., eds. *The Environment in Question: Ethics and Global Issues.* London and New York: Routledge, 1991.

Daly, Herman E., ed. *Economics, Ecology, Ethics.* San Francisco: Freeman Pub., 1980.

Dower, Nigel, ed. *Ethics and Environmental Responsibility.* Brookfield, VT: Avebury Pub., 1989.

Eisenbud, Merril. *Environment, Technology and Health: Human Ecology in Historical Perspective.* New York: New York Univ. Press, 1978.

Engel, J.R. *Environmental Ethics: Sustainable Development and the Human Future.* Belhaven Press, 1990.

Engel, J.R., Engel, J.G., eds. *Ethics of Environment and Development: Global Challenges, International Response.* Tucson: Univ. of Arizona Press, 1990.

Feldman, David Lewis. *Water Resources Management: In Search of an Environmental Ethic.* Baltimore: Johns Hopkins Univ. Press, 1991.

Fritsch, Albert J. et al. *Environmental Ethics: Choices for Concerned-Citizens.* Garden City, N.Y.: Anchor Press, 1980.

Glass, Bentley. *Science and Ethical Values.* Chapel Hill, N.C.: University of North Carolina Press, 1965.

136

Goodpaster, K.E., ed. *Ethics and Problems of the 21st Century*. Notre Dame, In: Univ. of Notre Dame Press.

Goodwin, Geoffrey, ed. *Ethics and Nuclear Deterrence*. New York: St. Martin's Press, 1982.

Gunn, Alastair, S. Vesilind, P. Aarne. *Environmental Ethics for Engineers*. Chelsea, MICH: Lewis Publishers, 1986.

Hargrove, Eugene C., ed. *Beyond Spaceship Earth: Environmental Ethics and the Solar System*. San Franciso: Sierra Club Books, 1986.

Hargrove, Eugene C. *The Animal Rights, Environmental Ethics Debate: The Environmental Perspective*. Albany, N.Y.: SUNY Press, 1992.

Hargrove, Eugene C. *Foundations of Environmental Ethics*. Englewood Cliffs, N.J.: Prentice Hall, 1989.

Hoffman, W. Michael, Frederick, Robert, Petry, Edward S., eds. *Business, Ethics and the Environment: The Public Policy Debate*. New York: Quorum Books, 1990.

Hoffman, W. Michael, ed. *The Corporation, Ethics and the Environment*. New York: Greenwood Press, 1990.

Johnson, Lawrence E. *A Morally Deep World: An Essay on Moral Significance and Environmental Ethics*. Cambridge and New York: Cambridge University Press, 1991.

Kealey, Daniel A. *Revisioning Environmental Ethics*. Albany, N.Y.: SUNY, Press, 1990.

Kranzberg, Melvin, ed. *Ethics in an Age of Pervasive Technology*. Boulder, COLO: Westview Press, 1980.

Maxey, Margaret. *Managing Environmental Risks: What Difference Does Ethics Make?*. St. Louis: Center for the Study of American Business, Washington University, 1990.

137

Mayo, D.G., Hollander, R.D., eds. *Acceptable Evidence: Science and Values in Risk Management.* New York: Oxford University Press, 1991.

McWhorter, LaDelle. *Heidegger and the Earth: Issues in Environmental Philosophy.* Lanham, MD: University Press of America, 1990.

Meeker, Joseph W. *The Comedy of Survival: In Search of an Environmental Ethic.* Finn Hill Publishers, 1980.

Mighetto, Lisa. *Wild Animals and American Environmental Ethics.* Tuscon: University of Arizona Press, 1991.

Miller, Alan S. *A Planet to Choose.* New York: Pilgrim Press, 1978.

Murphy, Charles M. *At Home on Earth: Foundations for a Catholic Ethic of the Environment.* New York: Crossroad Press, 1989.

Nash, Roderick. *The Rights of Nature: A History of Environmental Ethics.* Madison, WIS.: University of Wisconsin Press, 1989.

Parsons, Howard L. *Self, Global Issues and Ethics.* Amsterdam:Gruner, 1980.

Partridge, Ernest, ed. *Responsibilities to Future Generations: Environmental Ethics.* Buffalo, N.Y.: Prometheus Books, 1981.

Regan, Tom. *All That Dwell Therein: Animal Rights and Environmental Ethics.* Berkeley, CA: Univ. of California Press, 1982.

Regan, Tom, ed. *Earthbound: New Introductory Essays in Environmental Ethics,* 1st ed. Philadelphia: Temple University Press, 1984.

Rolston, Holmes. *Environmental Ethics: Duties to and Values in the Natural World*. Philadelphia: Temple University Press, 1988.

Rolston, Holmes. *Philosophy Gone Wild: Environmental Ethics*. Buffalo, N.Y.: Prometheus Books, 1989.

Scherer, D., Attig, T., eds. *Ethics and the Environment*. Englewood Cliffs, N.J.: Prentice Hall, 1983.

Scherer, Donald, ed. *Upstream/Downstream: Issues in Environmental Ethics*. Philadelphia: Temple University Press, 1990.

Schultz, Robert C., ed. *Ecological Consciousness*. Washington, D.C.: University Press of America, 1981.

Scoby, Donald R., ed. *Environmental Ethics: Studies of Man's Self Destruction*. Minneapolis: Burgess Pub. Co., 1971.

Shrader-Frechette, K.S. *Environmental Ethics*. Pacific Grove, CA: Boxwood Press, 1981.

Shrader-Frechette, K.S. *Science Policy, Ethics, and Economic Methodology: Some Problems of Technology Assessment and Environmental-Impact Analysis*. Dordrecht and Boston: D. Reidel Pub., 1985.

Swartzman, D., Liroff, R.A., Croke, K., eds. *Cost-Benefit Analysis and Environmental Regulations: Politics, Ethics and Methods*. Washington, D.C.: Conservation Foundation, 1982.

Taylor, Paul W. *Respect for Nature: A Theory of Environmental Ethics*. Princeton, N.J.: Princeton University Press, 1986.

Van De Veer, Donald, Pierce, Christine, eds. *People, Penguins and Plastic Trees: Basic Issues in Environmental Ethics.* Belmont, CA: Wadsworth Publishing Co., 1986.

JOURNALS (that publish work in environmental ethics)

AITIA, c/o Philosophy-Humanities, SUNY, Farmingdale, Farmingdale, N.Y. 11735

Agriculture and Human Values, c/o 243 ASB, University of Florida, Gainesville, Florida 32611

Environmental Ethics, c/o Department of Philosophy, University of Georgia, Athens, GA 30602

International Journal of Applied Philosophy, c/o Indian River Community College, Fort Pierce, Florida 33454-9003

Public Affairs Quarterly, c/o Department of Philosophy, University of Pittsburgh, Pittsburgh, PA 15260

Radical Philosophy, c/o Open University, Walton Hall, Milton Keynes, MK7 6AA, England

Research in Philosophy and Technology, c/o Department of Philosophy, University of Georgia, Athens, GA 30602